# So You Want to Start a Restaurant?

Revised Edition

Dewey A. Dyer

**A CBI Book**
Published by Van Nostrand Reinhold Company

A CBI Book
(CBI is an imprint of Van Nostrand Reinhold Company Inc.)

Copyright © 1981, 1971 by CBI Publishing Company, Inc.

Library of Congress Catalog Card Number 80-24278
ISBN 0-8436-2199-0

Printed in the United States of America
Designed by Katrine B. Stevens

Published by Van Nostrand Reinhold Company Inc.
135 West 50th Street
New York, New York 10020

Van Nostrand Reinhold Company Limited
Molly Millars Lane
Wokingham, Berkshire RG11 2PY, England

Van Nostrand Reinhold
480 La Trobe Street
Melbourne, Victoria 3000, Australia

Macmillan of Canada
Division of Gage Publishing Limited
164 Commander Boulevard
Agincourt, Ontario M1S 3C7, Canada

16 15 14 13 12 11 10 9 8 7 6 5 4 3 2

**Library of Congress Cataloging in Publication Data**

Dyer, Dewey A
    So you want to start a restaurant?

    Includes index.
    1. Restaurant management. I. Title.
TX911.3.M27D93     1981 647'.95'068     80-24278
ISBN 0-8436-2199-0

# Contents

iii

# Preface

The first edition of **So You Want to Start a Restaurant?** found its way into the hands of a wide variety of readers during the ten years since it first appeared. It has served its purpose well.

As an executive involved in development of a wide range of foodservice operations including market planning for new operations; supervising design and construction; and preopening, opening, and ongoing operations, I learned that while I could find many books dealing with menu planning, or French cooking, or accounting, there was not one that presented an overview of the business in a comprehensive or meaningful manner.

The most rewarding letters I have received from readers over the years have been from those who thanked me for providing an authoritative, insightful reference upon which to make the decision *not* to start their own restaurant. In these cases, people have been helped to avoid what might have been the biggest mistake of their lives. Too frequently, a lifetime of savings is spent on a long-cherished ambition to run a restaurant, and the result is disaster and disappointment.

In writing **So You Want to Start a Restaurant?** I hoped to remind readers who want to open a restaurant because they "cook a good gumbo" that a restaurant is a challenging combination of a manufacturing business and a retail outlet. It requires careful management and control of perishable inventories, production, people, and customers. Very few businesses include all of these variables as significant elements of success or failure!

Now, after ten years, much of the material in the first edition is dated. Costs have changed. Market emphasis has changed. Elements formerly of casual interest such as fuel, heating, and air conditioning, have suddenly loomed as major considerations. The time has come for a careful and thorough update. With this in mind, substantial effort and time have been expended to ensure that this revised edition will be the best and most comprehensive overview reference on the restaurant business. I trust that it will continue to be a useful book for individuals, entrepreneurs, and executives who may be contemplating an entry into the field without the benefit of significant prior experience.

Whatever your motivation to buy the book may have been, I believe it will light the way to the right decisions for you.

# The Plan
# is the Thing

# 1

Who has not been tempted, at one time or another, to try running a restaurant? There is probably no business that is more taken for granted or looks easier to run from the outside than the restaurant business. Yet, the highest rate of bankruptcies occurs in the restaurant business.

Many individuals who have spent a lifetime in the business, as cooks, chefs, or similar jobs, have cherished a lifelong ambition to build and operate their own restaurants. Many have finally realized their ambition and established a restaurant to have it last only a year or two, or perhaps three, before going under.

Properly approached, however, the restaurant business can be very rewarding and there are a great many individuals who, in succeeding in this activity, have found a creative outlet, financial independence, and a sense of true accomplishment.

If it is to succeed, the restaurant business, like any other, requires proper advance planning and a sound, businesslike approach.

It must be recognized that the restaurant business covers a whole spectrum of activities. Those who have spent a lifetime in the business will attest to the fact that one can succeed in a particular segment or type of restaurant operation, yet be a complete failure in another category of operation.

In many businesses, such as the hardware business or manufacturing, the problems do not call for nearly as high a degree of management ability as does restaurant operation.

A restaurant is a service business, appealing to the public. The many criteria relating to the customer that must be carefully considered and planned for will be pointed out in considerable detail as we progress.

Control of waste, sanitation, and the perishability of the product handled in this business all require astute buying and planning if waste and throwaway are not to be a restaurant's downfall.

## Segments of the Business

In general, the restaurant business is divided into these five major categories or segments:

1. At the top of the ladder is the *gourmet restaurant.* The true gourmet restaurant is rarely found in the United States today. Such an establishment emphasizes exquisitely prepared, sophisticated menu items, usually requiring highly skilled chefs who have liter-

2

ally spent a lifetime in apprenticeship and training in order to attain this skill.

Often these chefs are European trained. It is not uncommon to find that such an individual has begun his apprenticeship at the age of twelve or thirteen years and then spent ten, twelve, or fifteen years or even more attaining his present level of skill.

True gourmet restaurants often command a premium for their offerings and, therefore, are quite expensive and cater to an exclusive clientele.

2.   The *personality* or *character restaurant* covers the broadest range of establishments. It generally is identified by a specific personality or character, usually related to the atmosphere that has been developed for it.

Within this category falls the so-called "fine restaurant," featuring the "French service" that creates the atmosphere or character for this particular category.

Many "fine restaurants" are referred to by their owners as "gourmet restaurants" although they do not really fall into the gourmet category.

Other types of "personality" or "character" restaurants include the wide range of those that have rustic or wood paneled and leather interiors with carpeted floors, and that are built around Western, English Pub, Early American, or similar personality/character and decor themes. They also qualify as fine restaurants or family restaurants.

Another group within this category is the novelty restaurant; its special appeal is built around a unique approach or scheme that is unusual and, therefore, attractive.

3

The cost of food in the "personality" or "character" restaurant may range all the way from modest pricing and a semi-limited menu to a rather extensive menu with fairly expensive pricing.

3.  This category covers the *commercial restaurant* that, instead of emphasizing exquisite food preparation or personality, character, and atmosphere, primarily emphasizes relatively modest pricing and consistency. Such a restaurant is generally just a good, clean place to eat with "meat and potatoes" food, reasonably priced. Restaurants in this category are considered dependable since their food, pricing, and service are consistent and predictable.

4.  A category that has proliferated tremendously in the last several years is the *fast-food restaurant,* sometimes also categorically referred to as the "filling station." Restaurants in this group ordinarily specialize in a very limited menu, relatively inexpensively priced. They are situated in convenient locations, very much the type of location that a gasoline filling station would occupy providing a fast-in-and-out, and are modestly priced with limited offerings.

5.  The final restaurant segment we might best designate as *cafeterias;* they may be either public or private.

Cafeterias are similar to the fast-food establishment in that they feature modest pricing; however, in contrast, they are usually situated in high density locations, concentrate on the service of midday meals, depend on a degree of self-service, and provide a wider range of menu. The private sector of cafeteria operations covers those found in industrial plants, office buildings, and other such workplaces. These have as their mission the service of employee meals for specific working populations.

4

Usually a person who wants to go into the restaurant business has a certain type of restaurant in mind. To be successful, the new entrepreneur must first identify that segment of the overall business into which this type of restaurant falls. Then it's important to evaluate the manner in which the restaurant will be operated against the criteria for that segment of the business as well as against the expected competition in the area he wishes to serve.

# Where Will You Find Your Customer?

# 2

In order to structure your restaurant format effectively, you must first consider whom you will serve. Just what is the nature of the customer? And where may this customer be found?

Generally speaking, we are in a time of impressive growth and significant change. Looking ahead, we may expect personal income to increase by about 50 percent and individual spending power by about 40 percent by the end of the decade. Several very significant changes are taking place in our environment.

Children born during the post war baby boom have just entered their thirties; the level of education and its scope has increased measurably and there is a significant trend of the population to the suburbs. The effects of these factors in bringing about change in the next ten years will be far greater than the change which has been experienced in any comparable period in the history of the United States.

It is also very obvious to any individual living today that significant changes in our social values, as well as our hopes and ambitions, are under way. The economy of this nation has expanded at an average annual rate of about 4 percent since the end of World War II. As a record number of young people born immediately after 1946 came into the labor market, the labor force expanded at a record rate. However, just as the rate of population expansion went through a decline in the latter half of the 1960s, so will there be a decline in the rate of expansion within the labor market in the middle and late 1980s.

It can be expected that during the next five to ten years the economy will be subjected to major shocks, as attempts are made to cope with inflation, and the impact of inflation is felt in food costs, labor costs, and so on. The line between success and failure remains thin indeed, particularly for entrepreneurs, and even thinner for those entrepreneurs who are working with limited capital.

Adverse impact of high discount rates imposed by the Federal Reserve Board and attendant high interest rates often make the most profitable effort that of debt avoidance. Recessionary cycles have become more frequent, and the economic situation will remain precarious for some time to come. Until the problem of balance of payments, which creates dollars abroad that come back to haunt us, is solved, and while the discrepancy is exacerbated by the higher costs of imported goods in the United States, the economic picture will remain uncertain.

Energy will continue to be a major consideration, as its cost continues to increase. Energy conservation by appropriate construction techniques and by careful selection of equipment, will have to be a major consideration for the foreseeable future. In many instances the planner of a restaurant might well opt for building within a shopping center as opposed to constructing a free standing building. By making such a choice, one keeps construction costs down, preserves energy, and finds ready customers in the shoppers who frequent the area. More on these points later.

Years ago we heard a great deal of talk about the population explosion, so much as to almost cloud the fact that during the period of 1950 to 1960 it had all but leveled off, and in the period of 1960 to date the rate has declined markedly.

A resurgence of population growth did take place in the early 1970s as the war babies began to build families of their own; however, this increase was not comparable to that experienced in the years immediately following World War II.

As a matter of fact, the number of children born in the last four or five years is down about one-third from the peak level that occurred in the mid-fifties.

Another consideration of import is the fact that because of the number of young adults now in their twenties, the number of homes with children will expand most impressively during the next ten years. When we analyze these facts in terms of establishing the potential for customers, it is interesting to note that the size of various age groups in the child population will vary. Some groups will expand, others will decline.

For example, the number of preschool children has been declining since about 1965 although, with the rising births in the 1970s, it has tended to increase again. However, the number of teens can be expected to go down in the next ten years, as the birth decline which took place in the latter half of the 1960s begins to show up at that age level.

9

## A Younger Crowd

As part of this overall picture, the change in the age mix of adults is also very significant. In the next ten years or so, adults under 35 years of age will become half again as many. The difficult years of the 1930s resulted in a decrease in births during that period, with the result that the number of people in the 35 to 54 age bracket will not expand at all, while persons now 55 and over will increase at a rate a bit faster than that of the total population.

This growth pattern has very significant economic consequences since in the late 1960s, for example, 55 percent of the population was of working age; whereas ten years later the working age group was nearer 60 percent of the total population.

We can anticipate, therefore, a more rapid pace in the formation of families and a sizable increase in the formation of households (which includes families as well as individuals living alone or with persons other than relatives).

The population of households headed by persons under thirty-five will grow more than twice as fast as the total population; therefore, a greater percentage of total spending power will be from young homes in the 1980s. This is most significant since in recent years less than one-fourth of the personal income could be attributed to households headed by persons under thirty-five years of age. The younger consumer, therefore, will be more important in tomorrow's marketplace.

On the other hand, since income generally improves with experience and age, it might be expected that about two-thirds of the discretionary spending power will be concentrated in the age bracket from 35 to 65, although that group will account for only about half of the households.

10

## New Educational Levels

At the present time about one out of every five adults has had some exposure to college; and about one out of ten has completed at least a four-year college curriculum. In ten years, one out of every four adults will have been to college and about 15 percent will have earned a degree. Paralleling this, there will be a sizable increase in the number of people with full high school education, quite a significant factor when one considers that at this time fewer than one out of every three adults has attained the level of a high school diploma.

This indicates, since better schooling generally means better pay, that a larger share of the spending power will be coming from homes with a higher level of education. It also indicates that the occupational mix of the nation's labor force will undergo a change.

Because of the rapid advances in technology, the proliferation of scientific industries, the fantastic growth of the computer industry, and the growing complexity of modern business requiring administrative abilities, the need for white-collar employees is being greatly intensified.

At the same time, technology has resulted in rising productivity, requiring relatively fewer workers on the assembly lines. At the end of World War II, for example, the number of blue-collar workers was about 15 percent greater than the number of white-collar workers; whereas, currently, about 30 percent more persons are employed in white-collar occupations than in blue-collar jobs; and in ten years it is expected that about 60 percent more people will be in white-collar occupations.

11

## Where Do They Live?

The customer with discretionary spending power, essential to the successful development of a restaurant, will tend to be a white-collar professional or technical worker in the age bracket of 34 to 54, who has had some college and has a couple of children in elementary school.

Now that we have an idea of what this customer is like, we should next be concerned with where we might find him.

In the last twenty-five years there has been a tremendous movement of the population to the suburbs. Suburbs generally have been growing twice as fast as the total population and over five times as fast as the cities. While the population of cities will tend to inch up somewhat in the next ten years, the population of suburbs is expected to continue its present rate of growth. This means that, in relative terms, there will be a decline in the number of people residing in cities as a percentage of the total population.

The percentage of people living in non-metropolitan or rural areas will remain about the same. The big growth will continue to take place in the suburbs and in smaller communities more remote from metropolitan centers.

As we put the various facts together, we begin to see not only what the preferred customer will be like but where he probably will be living.

### The Energy Factor

Energy is another important factor that will determine where your customers will be found. The jury is still out on the projected impact of fuel availability on the living habits of the overall population. Yet there is now emerging a real probability that we will see a resurgence of inner city renewal in the future, certainly until relatively cheap alternative sources of fuel for locomotion are developed. The platform for meaningful urban renewal aimed at attracting middle-income as well as affluent people back to the cities is now fairly obvious.

It is undoubtedly also true that the general trends of population movement will continue for some time toward the Sun Belt and the West. However, the problems which attend growth in areas that are not prepared to assimilate growth efficiently cause us to judge that this will be a fairly temporary trend. People who flee to the South to escape the expense of long, cold winters, soon learn that these expenses are quickly replaced by other costs. New water systems, sewers, and other municipal systems and services, together with the heavy cost of air conditioning, can result in unforeseen financial burdens for newcomers. The single most significant element affecting this entire situation will continue to be availability and cost of petroleum base fuels and natural gas.

In short, when considering a location, one must consider much more than the current demographics. One must carefully study these demographics to make some hard judgments about how they might be changing in the three to ten years following your projected opening.

## These People Eat Out

The next step is to analyze spending power. It is interesting to note that average family earnings in the suburbs and smaller communities are now gaining ground on average family earnings in the city. Therefore, a disproportionately large and rising share of income will be found in suburban homes. Although the recent return of population pockets to the cities has apparently clouded the point, the return to the cities has not even begun to offset the exodus of previous years.

In 1977 about 29 percent of personal income was found in central cities, 42 percent was attributable to suburbs, and

13

rural areas accounted for another 20 percent. This has redistributed to 20 percent of family income in central cities, 55 percent in suburbs, and 25 percent in so-called rural areas.

By 1990, solutions to some of the social problems which are directly related to skill acquisition will cause personal income to be more equitably distributed among the populations (more income in the lower socio-economic levels) and this, together with distribution of population, will bring about a condition whereby more like 35 percent of personal income will be found in central cities, 55 or 60 percent in suburbs and small cities and towns, and the remainder in rural areas.

The significance of these trends is not so much a factor affecting the need for restaurants, but very much a factor with respect to the kinds of restaurants needed, for example, fast food versus theme, and so on.

It is expected that 70 percent of these suburban families will have average annual earnings in excess of $18,000. Suburban areas will account for well over 40 percent of the nation's families in the country, almost half of the people in the twenty-five to forty-five age bracket; over half of the college trained people; over half of the executive and managerial as well as professional population; and nearly 60 percent of the nation's discretionary income.

# What Will the Customer of the Future Demand?

# 3

We have identified a profile of the typical family restaurant customer and where he may be found. Next to be considered are the geographical implications with regard to population as well as the trend with respect to married women who work outside the home and their relation to customer demand.

Every year about 3½ percent of the population moves from one state to another. This is a rather sizable amount of moving about and, surprisingly enough, the motivation generally reduces itself largely to four overall influences: (1) moving away from the farm; (2) moving to areas having contract awards; (3) moving to take advantage of boom growth in certain specialized industries; (4) moving to a mild climate.

Since the factors affecting migration will continue to have approximately the same influence, the areas that have

15

expanded most rapidly in the past can be expected to continue to do so in the future. However, a tendency towards equalization of income from one region to another has resulted in spending power increasing faster in areas where the income has been below average than in those where it has been above average.

At present, less than 30 percent of all families have earnings of $10,000 or more; but in ten years it is expected that about 55 percent of families will exceed this level of income, measured in current dollars.

In addition, although today households receiving an income of less than $5,000 per year amount to about 30 percent of the total, in the next ten years this percentage will be approximately halved.

An important factor which will contribute to this change in the distribution of income will be the continued movement of women into the labor force. Ten years from now the number of married women who are employed outside the home will be about 25 percent greater than at present.

This trend will have sociological implications; it will also have specific implications in terms of the restaurant market and, of course, will contribute vitally to sustaining the family unit in a higher income bracket.

As we have seen, both the age mix and income distribution are undergoing significant changes. Since these factors are by far the most important that affect spending, we can anticipate that the pattern of consumer spending ten years from now will be changed.

Households in the age group from twenty-five to forty-five, with earnings of $10,000 or more, will undoubtedly represent the fastest growing sector of the market. In ten years this sector will be responsible for about 40 percent of all spending, as opposed to 25 percent at present. Since at the same time

16

the total income will be increasing, the demands of this particular segment of the market will substantially more than double.

As the fortunes of the average family improve, a smaller percentage of its resources will be required to meet the basic needs of food, clothing, and shelter, and an increasing proportion will become available for those things that make for a full and better life. Consequently, a larger proportion of spending will go for those items that fall into the spectrum of luxury goods and services. It is expected that the number of dollars available for spending for food away from home, therefore, will be greater.

To establish a "feel" as to those segments of the restaurant industry which offer the greatest potential for success, as opposed to those in which success is perhaps less likely, the factors discussed in this chapter and in the preceding chapters, should be related to the various segments.

In order to assess the potential for success, we must look at this hypothetical customer and examine the various reasons why he chooses to eat away from home.

# Why Do People Eat Out?

# 4

Since the reason for eating out affects the amount of money spent and the type of establishment to which an individual goes, the typical customer's reasons for eating out must be understood. They break down into five basic categories:

## The Working Situation

The most obvious reason why people eat out is because they are employed in a situation or location that makes eating lunch at home impractical. The types of establishments that answer this need are the employee cafeterias, vending machine installations, or similar facilities situated at the place of employment.

The employed person may also eat in a commercial restaurant or public cafeteria located in the neighborhood of his place of employment.

Whatever the chosen location, the employee is primarily seeking a sustaining meal at a minimum cost. Average checks in this category then must range somewhere between $1.65 and $2.50 for the great bulk of hourly employees.

In the case of higher level, supervisory, middle-management, and executive employees, a concern for economy also exists although the average check can go up to $3.50 or $3.75, and in occasional instances, even a bit higher.

The economic limitations imposed by these check averages necessarily create some limitations on what can be offered within such a price structure. A second element that creates limitations upon what can be offered in this price range is the eating habits of the various types of people.

In very simple terms, these eating habits break down into three broad categories:

1. Employees who work at heavy manual labor and in blue-collar occupations. These individuals either carry lunch in a lunchbox or bag or are interested in a rather substantial hot meal at minimum cost. The employees in this group who eat out, then, are normally anticipating a reasonable range of selection with a hot and fairly substantial meal, such as meat, vegetable, and potatoes.

2. Clerical, office, and technical employees. Individuals in this group tend to eat lighter meals and to be much more weight conscious. In the technical occupations particularly, there is a tendency to drink more coffee and to eat very light meals at midday, such as a light sandwich; soup and sandwich; salads or light snacks.

20

3.  Middle-management and upper middle-management. These are people who like to combine a hot meal at a reasonable cost with a moment away from the desk or a moment of midday relaxation. Lunch for this group often has a social or companionship aspect with two or more such people lunching together. This social benefit makes them want more and makes them willing to pay a little more for what they want.

## The Convenience Decision

Another reason why people eat out can be classified as the "convenience decision." Convenience decisions generally develop from two situations.

a.  The need to eat while traveling

b.  Those situations when people just feel that they'd like to get out or don't want to bother with cooking, so they say, "Let's eat out tonight."

Each of these convenience decisions must be analyzed separately because, surprisingly enough, each tends to demand a different type of service.

When making the convenience decision to eat while traveling, the individual is normally interested in a modest meal at modest pricing. The traveling customer will also tend to choose a restaurant that is conveniently accessible and where the surroundings and the quality of the food are predictable.

Because this is so, major chain operations that have established a public image have a definite competitive advantage in appealing to travelers. Snack shops or dining rooms in conjunction with motels, hotels, and similar facilities also have a competitive advantage. The individual entrepreneurial effort to capture this market usually cannot compete successfully in this market.

In the "Let's eat out tonight" category of convenience decisions, demand is apt to vary according to the economic status of the individual involved.

In the lower-income brackets and the lower range of the middle-income brackets, the convenience decision will normally be met by the fast-food "filling station" type of operation, usually identified as the local, quick service hamburger or chicken-in-the-basket spot, pizza palace, or similar establishment. Normally, people in this category will be concerned with getting an adequate supply of food at a minimum cost.

This is a market that has been and continues to be thoroughly exploited by the proliferation of franchise food operations categorized in Chapter 1 as "filling stations."

As customers move up the economic ladder, getting into the $10,000–$15,000 per year income range and higher, they not only want the sort of convenience described above but also are willing to pay a small premium for an added degree of comfort and/or atmosphere.

In response to these requirements some franchise and entrepreneurial operations have developed formats offering somewhat greater menu variety. The hamburger is served in a pleasant atmosphere but at a premium price for hamburger.

The hamburger that might be purchased in the fast-food hamburger franchise chain for 25¢ or so and in the sit-down franchise chain or similar operation for 35¢ or 45¢ now becomes a hamburger priced in the 90¢ to $1.65 range. These price increases are due to inflation of costs of food, and pressures to provide service on china, in a sit-down atmosphere, and in improved surroundings. This trend is partially in response to necessity brought on by inflation and need for surroundings which make payment of higher prices more acceptable.

For customers in the $15,000 and higher salary range, the convenience decision usually leads to a meal in a modestly priced family restaurant because, again, at this income level the people are willing to pay still more and in return they want a more rounded selection and more elaborate presentation.

There is a definite overlapping between convenience decisions and the "night out" and "special event." This "overlapping" is based on economic status. The modestly priced family restaurant that might represent a place to go on the "night out" for customers in the lower half of the middle-income brackets, would, at the same time, be the destination resulting from a convenience decision made by customers in the upper half of the middle-income bracket.

This is a very subtle but important point since the structure of menu and pricing, if astutely evolved, can cause the range of your effort to encompass two separate and adjacent markets instead of restricting it to the narrower zone of an individual market.

## The Night Out

Another reason why people eat out can be classified as the "night out." This is a little different from the convenience decision in that a bit more in the way of comfort, atmosphere, and/or entertainment is anticipated. The requirements, of course, will vary according to the economic status of the particular group of customers.

An analysis of the habits of families with children indicates that families with children, on a national average, go out to eat in a sit-down restaurant approximately ten times a year. Their expenditure in this activity ranges from about $150 to $200 per year, with the higher amount spent by families with four children or more, and the lower amount by families with one or two children at younger ages.

The family customer in this category will probably have children under twelve years of age and will probably anticipate eating for an average, per person, of between $5.00 and $8.00. Because the "night out" is a special event they will look for attentive service and a reasonable menu selection.

In the upper-income range, the "night out" will move out of the family restaurant and into the fine restaurant or gourmet restaurant since the people in the upper range are looking for finer food, more comfort, more service, and possibly entertainment; and they can afford to pay for the combination. The majority of customers planning a night out will fall into this category.

Analysis reveals that of the money spent in restaurants by families with children, about 14 percent will be for children's meals and orders of such items as chopped sirloin, hamburger, or some variation of these.

Analysis of menus from a wide range of restaurants reveals that, when frequency of selection among adults is taken into consideration, somewhere in the area of 70 percent of the individual selections made in the restaurant will be for beef items. These include the various types of steaks, roast beef, chopped sirloin, hamburgers, corned beef, brisket of beef, and account for about 70 percent of the sales.

Since beef tends to be a high cost item, what might appear to be a high average check is really not so high when one considers the amount of money people normally spend on the night out. Maintaining a profitable check average becomes more difficult to accomplish when customers are primarily made up of family groups.

The challenge of providing menu diversity becomes greater as efforts to maintain the overall cost of food are tested by increasing price pressure upon staple items such as beef. The extent to which this challenge is met can have great impact upon the success or failure of individual operations.

## A Special Event

Another reason why people go out to eat we would classify as the "special event." The special event can celebrate such occasions as the grandparents visiting; an anniversary; a child's birthday party; or a special night out together with friends.

In the case of the special event, people are expecting a little more because they are in more of a celebrating mood and are willing to spend a little more.

Following the rationale provided above, we see that those people in the lower half of the middle-income range, and some from the lower end of that range, would normally go to the type of family restaurant just described; whereas people from the upper end of the middle-income range would go to the fine restaurant or the gourmet restaurant.

## When They're Away from Home

There is another category: customers living away from home. This market normally falls into a variety of categories which overlap. Living away from home, for example, involves the college student who would eat in the student union or college cafeteria, supplementing this with the "filling station" type of restaurant operation. Also included in this category is the person living in a residential hotel who would usually eat in the hotel dining room but, for the reasons previously described would sometimes go to a restaurant.

People traveling, staying in a hotel or motel, will usually eat breakfast in the hotel dining room or coffee shop but will tend to select their other eating places for reasons described previously.

## Growth Markets

Examining the several reasons why people eat out helps to determine whether, as a market force, they represent a growth market or a declining market.

On examination, the industrial cafeteria and office building cafeteria will appear to be a declining business for a variety of reasons:

1. The shorter work day that will enable the individual to get by with a snack or a light carryover luncheon;

2. The tendency toward more and more white-collar and technical jobs and fewer blue-collar jobs because of automation in industry, with the result that the number of people who eat heavily (the blue-collar and manual laborers) are decreasing while the number of those who eat more lightly (white-collar and technical workers) is increasing.

3. Dispersal of business activities into the new cluster developments and the cost of construction in creating new plants that are contributing to a situation in which the in-plant feeding facility may be eliminated in favor of local supporting facilities that service a number of plants in a given area.

It is fairly common knowledge that most hotels and motels have done a less than desirable job in their dining facilities. While there are some situations where the entrepreneur can obtain a contract to provide dining facilities in a hotel, these opportunities are rare. The subject of hotel and motel dining rooms seems to require a great deal of study and inves-

26

tigation, and we will no doubt see a transitional change in these restaurants in the next few years.

There will be a great deal more emphasis on atmosphere and pricing and probably a trend toward a wider use of convenience foods in order to attain modest menu pricing by offsetting pyramiding labor costs and other food preparation expenses.

The franchising, convenience, and "filling station" activity will continue to grow because of several pressures favoring this type of establishment. Among them are:

1. Rapid, overall growth of population.

2. The tendency of more and more people to want to be individual proprietors of their own businesses.

3. The fact that many promoters, legitimate and questionable alike, recognize these two factors and are exploiting them very aggressively.

We will not cover the subject of franchising here. However, there are some excellent books on franchising, and anyone who is considering franchising should do some research on the subject and make certain that he is working with a well-established, reputable franchising organization before becoming involved.

Convenience roadside restaurants will experience great growth because of the imminent completion of the interstate highway program and the great proliferation of recreational travel. As noted earlier, many travelers, if not most, are looking for some identification which guarantees them consistency; therefore, the chain operator with an established reputation has a distinct advantage in this market.

Any effort to penetrate this market in competition with the company having an established image requires very, very careful selection of site and equally careful design of the building in order to establish a conspicuous, favorable image which correlates with the overall image demanded by travelers.

Selecting sites for roadside restaurants will require special analysis of travel patterns, which are bound to change and continue changing as the long-range impact of fuel shortages becomes more emphatic and permanent.

### Family Sit-Down Restaurants

The family sit-down restaurants will experience great expansion, primarily because of the rapid movement of people from the cities to the suburbs and the fact that at this time services such as this are relatively scarce in most suburban communities.

It is to be expected that as this fact is recognized, more and more major corporations will expend effort in this direction. However, since this type of restaurant falls into the family, personality, character, and atmosphere category, this is one field in which the individual entrepreneur can compete very effectively with a major corporation and, in many respects, has advantages over the corporation.

For the individual, then, it would appear that right now the chances of greatest success exist in the market segment characterized as the suburban, family, sit-down restaurant market.

Looking ahead to the next five years, however, the real probability of a trend back to the cities, or urban areas, must be considered. It would appear that a mixture of privately funded urban renewal, together with federally subsidized urban renewal may dramatically change the mix of construction in the inner cities. More medium-priced and luxury housing will no doubt be prevalent as people employed in the cities opt for city living and their demand is met with apartment and condominium construction adjacent to and within downtown business and financial centers.

# Menu Planning

# 5

Analysis of the major attitudes and spending habits of the customer brings us to the point of evaluating the type of menu that should be presented in order to maximize the appeal of a restaurant effort. While the full range of the menu can vary, and undoubtedly will vary, from one segment of the market to another, there are some basic elements that should be considered as a skeleton, so to speak, upon which to hang the muscle that will make up the finished menu.

We can begin by recognizing that the preference in seven out of ten instances in today's taste choices is for a beef selection. An effective menu, therefore, should have a good selection of beef which normally would include a good steak, appropriately priced, a medium-priced steak, a roast beef item, a chopped sirloin or similar item, and a hamburger or related item.

The roast beef item can be replaced by other varieties of beef such as pepper steak, sirloin tips with mushroom sauce, beef burgundy, beef goulash, a good old-fashioned beef stew, or a similar item.

Having established a basic structure with a full range in price from high to low, involving selections of beef, the menu next requires a fowl and a fish item and a meat item other than beef.

In building around the basic beef elements, there is a wide range of items from which to choose. Your choices will depend upon the nature of your restaurant, your preferences, and local tastes.

For example, the fowl item might be a Long Island duckling, a Rock Cornish game hen, half of a broiled chicken, half of a baked chicken or Southern fried chicken; while the fish item, depending upon the type of restaurant again, might be French fried shrimp, or shrimp De Jonge, poached salmon, swordfish steak, or the various types of filets. Your non-beef item could be breaded pork cutlet, or veal parmigiana.

In a good, fast moving, family neighborhood where small children are a factor, regardless of the personality and character of the restaurant, you can well include a spaghetti and meat sauce special, since this is always a good item that enjoys low food cost and high frequency of selection.

With the fundamentals of the main body of the menu established, we now look at the remainder of the menu. Here is where your showmanship and range of imagination really come into play. Consider the number of times that you have gone into a restaurant and seen the same old items staring you in the face from the top of the menu under the heading of "Appetizers." This is a place where you can make your offerings unusual. Appetizers should include at least one soup, preferably two (one light and one heavy).

Salads are often provided in a wide range or variety but again in the family type of restaurant it is more than adequate to have one good tossed or chef's salad and to provide a variety of dressings as the element of choice. The ingredients of a tossed salad can be varied from night to night to introduce a surprise element even though only one salad is served.

In the category of breads, it is very much preferred to establish some unique bread—perhaps a dark rye, muffins, or hot baking powder biscuits—and start off with this specialty instead of the usual basket of crackers wrapped in cellophane.

It also seems to add charm and a special element of service when bread is presented hot on a cutting board and with a small knife. This extra touch is interpreted by many customers as concern for their pleasure and comfort, and it pays dividends.

When you get down into the dessert column, you will find that in this age of weight consciousness desserts for the most part will be passed up. Supplementing the weight consciousness as a reason for passing up desserts, is the lack of originality in many dessert menus. How frequently you see under "Desserts" only ice cream, sherbet, sundaes, and pies; and the pies are the usual mass-produced bakery selections.

There are many, many interesting and exciting individual items which can be easily developed on a practical basis for desserts. It really is necessary to have only three or four selections.

It is very desirable, however, to put some imagination and showmanship into these selections so that they become a high point in terms of color and excitement as well as something to talk about as one finishes the meal.

## Drink Selections

In choosing wines, customers generally find that a house wine is easy to order. Where wine is to be served (except in the really fine restaurants), the offerings can be limited to a good red wine and a good white wine, both of a caliber that satisfies the connoisseur and yet is not beyond the capacity of the wine drinker who is not a regular or a connoisseur.

Wines like a dark rose, perhaps Portuguese, or a white rhine wine such as Liebfraumilch, make excellent house wines, providing the compromise suggested above.

More and more restaurant operators are also learning that a varied inventory of liquor is not necessary for the operation of a comprehensive bar; one can operate a very adequate bar with the liquor selections limited to seven or eight. This bar would include a light or a dark scotch, a Canadian or blend, a bourbon, a gin, a vodka, and a straight whiskey.

By far the most frequent selection in cocktails will be martinis, with the vodka martini making great headway and now almost holding its own with the gin martini; next in preference comes the Manhattan.

Depending upon the part of the country, the third most frequent choice will tend to be a "woman's drink." With some variation for regional preference, it will be either a daiquiri or a sour, such as a whiskey sour.

Hot-weather drinks, while not representing a significant part of the total bar sales, will normally gravitate to the collins, Tom or John, and the gimlet.

Also, unless the operation qualifies as a fine or gourmet restaurant, it is not really necessary to provide more than two choices of beer, normally a light and a medium heavy.

## Child Pleasers

Since families tend to select restaurants that are conscious of children and that do special things for them, it is well worth the effort to dress up children's drinks with a lemon slice over the edge of the glass or a cherry dropped into the glass. This takes very little extra effort; yet it gets a very fine reception at the customer's table.

Some restaurants go further and provide special little souvenir items for children such as a trinket for the child who leaves his plate clean, or a consideration for the child who brings in a report card with all "As" or any one of a variety of similar promotions.

A variety of promotions is not really required, but be sure the promotions chosen show thoughtfulness as well as genuine interest in and awareness of the child.

## Fast Food

As we move from the family restaurant into the fast-food or filling station, we get into a category which, by definition, is fairly inflexible. In other words, the hamburger houses pretty much limit themselves to hamburgers and the pizza houses to pizza. These operations will undoubtedly add one or two other items in order to allow for a choice; this is sound thinking.

The format of the fast-food operation is such that any menu extension should be limited to one or two side selections. Several years ago many restaurants responded to the pancake fad, and pancake houses sprang up about the country for a short time. The initial reception was excellent, but the format was not properly thought out from a marketing point of view, and these restaurants soon found themselves in serious difficulty.

These problems occurred primarily because there is a limit to the number of times a customer wants to go back for pancakes, however wide the variety may be; yet the economics of these operations was built on a food cost based on pancakes, and it is very low. As business began to drop off, somewhat in desperation the pancake houses began to expand their menus to include a variety of other items. This measure resulted in a disruption of the cost relationships and precipitated a great many new problems for these restaurants.

Restaurants today have moved into other fad fields, such as pizza, and it is this author's view that as time passes these restaurants will also go through the same type of tradition that the pancake houses experienced.

To be successful in the long pull, it is necessary to think through your market approach thoroughly, then structure your image and approach to give your operation staying power.

## Convenience Foods

There is developing in the marketplace a greater and greater awareness of foods identified as "convenience foods," and it is interesting to note that more and more of the large commercial restaurant operators are relying heavily upon convenience foods in order to obtain consistency and to reduce preparation cost.

The restaurant business is on the threshold of a convenience food revolution; the principal factor holding it back at this time is the unwillingness of people who have been in the business for many years to accept these convenience foods and the types of equipment with which they may be processed efficiently.

As younger people get into the business and as the keenness of competition, accompanied by the profit squeeze generated by rising costs across the board, continues to grow, the utilization of convenience foods will become much more widespread.

34

For this reason, perhaps, a short discussion of convenience foods is appropriate while we are discussing menu. First of all, many people regard convenience foods as precooked, frozen items; however, it should be pointed out that the term "convenience foods" really is intended to convey the thought that the work of preparing the food has been done elsewhere and the food is now available for serving with a minimum amount of handling.

One example of this type of convenience food is the packaged sliced bread that people now use, thus avoiding the necessity for the long and laborious process of baking bread at home. Another widely accepted form of convenience food is canned soup. Today many canned selections not only provide a wide variety but also ensure consistency and quality. The preparation of a zesty soup need now take only minutes, as opposed to the hours consumed in producing this item prior to its advent in convenience packaging.

Other examples are bakery pies, cakes, canned vegetables, and frozen vegetables. In processing canned and frozen vegetables, the shelling, cleaning, and much of the cooking is done ahead of time so that the package-to-plate transition is very short, requiring a minimum of time and effort. Many of the foods used in restaurants now are convenience foods but are not so regarded even by the restaurateurs.

The convenience foods that are on the threshold of expanded use are the more comprehensive assembled items. More and more restaurants are using pre-cut and pretrimmed steaks, prepackaged hamburgers, precooked turkey pies, meat pies, pot pies, and other combination dishes.

As this market expands and the built-in resistance fades, the variety and quality of foods available will proliferate very rapidly and the skills required to prepare food for an average operation will diminish in proportion.

The wide-awake individual in the restaurant business will keep an alert eye and an open mind with regard to this development; he will have very little patience with the built-in resistance to modern equipment, such as the Foster Recon unit, produced by Foster Refrigeration Company, or the various modifications of infrared and microwave in conjunction with convection heat that are moving into the marketplace.

# Determining
# Building
# Requirements

# 6

Having determined the type of restaurant you want to operate, the next decision is to determine what kind of building should house this restaurant. There are two fundamental approaches: (a) the free-standing building; and (b) the remodeled adapted building.

The choice as to the type of building will, to some extent, depend upon the type of restaurant to be constructed. As an example, those restaurants that can be described as commercial restaurants will be situated in high density, urban areas.

Since, for the most part, all of the available land has been occupied in the high density, urban areas and the cost of buying land with an existing building and then tearing down the building to construct a new, free-standing building is prohibi-

37

tive, the approach in the high density, urban area probably should be to remodel an existing building.

To put the problem of remodeling on a sound basis, first determine the high density area and then, having identified the location, seek out an appropriate building for remodeling.

Financing this effort can follow one of two courses: (a) remodeling a building with the cost of remodeling to be carried by the restaurateur who has rented or leased the building for a long period of time, preferably a minimum of ten years, with appropriate renewal options; or (b) remodeling to be agreed upon between the lessor and the restaurateur, with the lessor completing the remodeling and including the cost of remodeling in the rental charge.

Obviously, if the restaurateur is operating with limited finances, the second approach will require much less capital at the outset, but it will result in a premium in rent charges over a long period of time.

In approaching the actual design, the restaurateur should construct a pro forma statement covering the proposed restaurant business. He should determine the break-even point and the optimum seating capacity needed to provide for the return that he is seeking. As a rule of thumb, the restaurant planner can utilize 20 sq. ft. for each seat to be provided, except in the case of fine restaurants or gourmet restaurants, where 25 or 30 sq. ft. are necessary to provide for a less compact seating arrangement.

Since the steps to be followed subsequently will be more or less the same in either instance, we will use the 20 sq. ft. seating example and follow through on the planning process by way of illustration.

Let's assume that it is the intention of a restaurateur to provide seating for 160 people in the area where he anticipates peak luncheon business. The wise planner will assume a single seating for luncheon business; that is, he will not plan on turning over his seats more than once during the luncheon period.

Accordingly, 160 seats at 20 sq. ft. per seat will require approximately 3200 sq. ft. of space. Next, he must provide for the preparation and storage areas and other back-up facilities. If he intends to take advantage of convenience foods and modern techniques of kitchen processing, he may use a kitchen and storage area equal to approximately one-third of the space allocated to seating or, in this case, about 1100 sq. ft.

In seeking a building for remodeling, the restaurateur then will be looking for a building with between 5000 and 6000 sq. ft. of floor space. Assuming that the floor space is on one floor he will require a building approximately 60 ft. by 100 ft.

The design of the building remodeling plan will break down into three fundamental elements: (1) exterior; (2) public areas: dining rooms, public restrooms, and so forth; and (3) food preparation and storage areas.

Too often, restaurants have been designed using a packaging engineering approach: the various elements of equipment, furniture, and fixtures that traditionally make up a restaurant are packaged into the space involved without consideration for the flow of material through the restaurant.

This approach should not be used, since it can well add a minimum of an additional 1000 sq. ft. to the area required, as opposed to the area needed when the operation is designed on the basis of a diagram showing flow of material.

## Design for Flow of Material

Using this approach the designer should begin by charting the flow of material, starting with the receiving of the various products to be handled, then the preparation of these products, and from there to the serving of the products or their distribution to waitresses and waiters, then finally, the flow of the products to the tables occupied by the customers.

A return flow for garbage and soiled dishes, as well as a traffic flow of service personnel and customers, must also be superimposed on the diagram.

Having created such a flow diagram or pattern, you are now prepared to assemble the various elements of storage equipment, preparation equipment, tables, chairs, and other items around the diagram in the most efficient manner possible.

In analyzing the flow of materials, it should be recognized that the receiving end of the diagram must provide space and facilities for receiving a variety of items that cannot all be treated in the same way. These items fall into three general categories: (1) dairy products and produce, which require a particular type of storage and must be processed through a pantry; (2) fresh or frozen vegetables which, in turn, will have to be prepared and cooked, arriving at the preparation area to be combined with the other items which go onto the plate to be served; (3) meat items which require a special type of storage and preparation as well as particular handling in cooking.

These three categories of products follow their own pattern of handling, all arriving at a single point to be assembled on the plate, and from there passed to the service personnel, who will transport them to the customers' tables.

Also important to table service is the availability and accessibility of beverages, including soft drinks, milk, coffee, tea, and, where appropriate, alcoholic beverages.

A typical flow diagram illustrating the complexities of the situation is provided on pages 72 and 73.

Because of the specialized nature of the area, a separate

chapter is included for discussion of the kitchen design and equipment, pages 67 to 80.

The exterior of the building should be distinctive, attractive, and should convey an image of wholesome hospitality. The procedure for establishing a building face is relatively easy, with the cost and materials prime factors in most buildings situated in urban, high density areas. The result is limited only by the imagination and ingenuity of the designer or planner.

When providing for the customer area or public areas, four simple elements must be coordinated:

1.  The entry and holding area for handling some stackup of customers waiting for tables;

2.  Cashier and checking area, providing sufficient coat storage, particularly in areas where inclement weather is a factor;

3.  Restrooms;

4.  Dining area.

## Where Costs Soar

In developing restaurants of this kind there are two places where builders invariably waste money or spend a great deal more money than is necessary to achieve the desired results. These are the kitchen area and the decor of the dining area. The materials and motif selected for decor can have a dramatic impact upon the cost of finishing off the interior of a restaurant dining area.

The most successful are those that are kept simple and in which atmosphere is achieved by artistic innovations in the utilization of simple materials such as wood paneling, wall

41

brackets, paintings, draperies, table arrangement, and dining room arrangement.

## Suburban Construction

As one examines the available markets and takes a look at what is happening in these markets in terms of customer preference, location of customers, spending habits, and so forth, it is much more likely that a restaurant facility will be planned for the suburban location. This type of location presents an entirely unique set of problems.

In the suburban location the free-standing building is a good deal more desirable, and, in many cases, an absolute necessity since appropriate buildings suitable for effective remodeling are much less prevalent.

In approaching the problem of building a freestanding structure, then, the first consideration will be the location of a site.

In suburban areas, sites that are appropriate for this type of activity can be quite expensive (from $40,000 to $250,000 depending upon the area of the country) and can present a number of problems before planners even get to the building itself.

The first problem, which should be obvious, is that of proper zoning.

When searching for a site for your restaurant, early consideration should be given to those appropriate areas that are zoned for commercial use or that are zoned for a use requiring more stringent control than does commercial use, such as light industry. Such zoning facilitates the problems of obtaining, through local zoning or planning board authorities, a special use permit or variance.

## Site Size

Again, assuming that the restaurant is to accommodate seating for 150 to 200, the need is for a freestanding building with an area of between 5000 and 6000 sq. ft.

The local building codes and zoning codes will then have to be checked to determine sideline and frontline setbacks, the distance required by local law, as a matter of zoning control, for a building to be set back from the street and from the side boundaries of the lot.

Based on the sideline requirements, determine the number of square feet of land space that will be required on your site in order to meet these restrictions.

If you have 200 ft. of frontage with a 50 ft. setback requirement, this will consume another 10,000 sq. ft. of ground area. This, combined with the building, results in a necessary total of about 15,000 sq. ft. of land.

The next consideration will be roadway or driveways in and out, and appropriate parking. Depending upon jurisdiction, it will cost between $1.00 and $3.00 per sq. ft. to prepare a parking lot area, and the area required for one automobile will be approximately 260 to 300 sq. ft. (allowing for access driveways and area taken up by light standards, signs, and other unavoidable lost space).

If the restaurant is going to provide parking for 50 cars, another 13,000 sq. ft. is required, making the minimum requirement, based upon the various footage needs discussed thus far, 28,000 to 30,000 square feet.

Such a lot size is approximately three fourths of an acre and, when unavoidable loss of space is taken into consideration as well as rear setbacks and sideline setbacks and accessibility for receiving and deliveries, a minimum practical lot size for a freestanding restaurant seating 150 to 200 people will prove to be one acre.

To give you a visual fix on this size, one acre is a parcel of land slightly larger than 200 feet square.

In determining this one-acre lot size it is assumed that utilities, especially sewage facilities, are available. If public sewage facilities are not available, then the alternative will be the development of a sewage treatment field that, in the example we are discussing would under average conditions, require approximately two-tenths of an acre of additional space.

Under "average conditions" means that water placed in a hole in the ground would percolate through the ground, disappearing from the hole in less than ten minutes. If a hole in the ground approximately two feet deep were filled with water and twenty minutes was required for the water to percolate from the hole, then the area required for the leaching or septic field would become four-tenths of an acre, or just under a half acre.

The precise parameters for solving this problem can be obtained by having a civil engineer or a sanitary engineer do what is called a "percolation test" on your property, thereby making a qualified and precise determination. Such an engineer will also be familiar with local codes and requirements for disposal fields and will be able to advise you accordingly. The cost of a percolation test, depending upon the part of the country involved, can run anywhere from $50 to $150.

Having determined the minimum size of the lot necessary to accommodate your requirements, following a pattern as has been described here, it is time to look at specific sites.

The first thing learned from looking at specific sites is that just any 1½-acre parcel of land will not necessarily be a desirable site for your restaurant. You will, therefore, have to establish some criteria for screening the sites that you will be viewing.

If your restaurant is to begin to attract customers quickly, it is fundamental that it be visible to the public; in other words, it must be situated on a site which exposes it to the view of a large number of people as they pass routinely during the course of their business or other travel activities. This makes it desirable for a site to be located on a main arterial highway, or a main commuter roadway, but not on a limited access highway.

We say "not on a limited access highway" because a limited access highway presents problems to people unfamiliar with the area as to how to get off such a road and get over to the restaurant after they see it.

If a site is available at or near the intersection of two main arterial highways, one running generally north and south and one running generally east and west, so much the better. At such a site the visibility is increased tremendously and with it the awareness of the public that your restaurant is in existence and ready to serve them.

## Budgeting Your Building

Having established the need to (1) build on a site of approximately 1½ acres and (2) put the free-standing building on an arterial system, then keeping in mind the previously determined restaurant format, you can determine the type of building to construct.

With the cost of construction having increased at the rate of approximately 1 percent per month for many years, the design selected for the building should lend itself to simple construction to hold costs within reasonable limits.

Here are some simple rules of thumb for use in realistically budgeting the cost of the building.

45

One rule of thumb, based upon 1980 costs, is to arrive at a total cost of building and land that will enable the restaurant operation to avoid the liability of carrying excessive real estate costs against its profit and loss statement. To do this, budget the land and building constructed and ready for opening, not to exceed $4500 for each customer seat to be provided.

In other words, the combined cost of land, design, construction, building, equipment, furnishing, and other necessities for a restaurant seating 160 customers should not exceed $720,000.

An alternate rule of thumb that can be used for planning purposes is that combined cost of facilities as described shall not exceed the amount anticipated as a conservative estimate of one year's sales.

Thus if our 160-seat restaurant is expected to do $720,000 per year in sales, it would be budgeted to cost no more than $720,000.

While the 160-seat restaurant used in this example is a sit-down, full service restaurant, the cost/yearly sales ratio would remain the same for an operator who had decided to construct a public, cafeteria-type restaurant or some other type of restaurant requiring a smaller seating area and with a smaller check average, because its requirement for higher traffic density would lead to a much more costly land site.

Whatever the combination of these variables—type of restaurant; value of site; value of building and equipment to be placed on the site; number of customers to be accommodated; and check average—they should result in a formula in which the facilities investment approximately equals a conservative estimate of one year's sales.

Here, in detail, are the costs that go into the development of such a building:

1.  Legal services will, of course, be required and, while special situations can change the amount required for such services, an adequate rule of thumb for budgeting should be $7500.

2.  Architectural design services may be purchased either with or without supervision of the construction process included. A viable estimate of cost for a proficient job of design and supervision of a building of the type discussed here would be $30,000.

3.  An additional $7500 should be provided to cover various fees for building permits, fees for tapping into utilities, the preparation of special materials, such as exhibits and plans, to be submitted to building inspectors, zoning boards, and other authorities.

The budgeted cost, then, for professional services associated with the development of an individual location such as the one we've described, together with various application fees which would be associated with these services, would be approximately $45,000.

It is entirely likely that in straightforward situations both architectural and legal services can be reduced somewhat from this estimate.

There remains approximately $675,000 for the purpose of buying land, constructing, and furnishing a building.

Certain elements of the building can be roughly budgeted in order to arrive at a control figure for the more variable items. For example, the kitchen equipment required can be placed under an allowance or budget figure of $80,000 which should be adequate. This is assuming, of course, the purchase of new equipment, and would include refrigeration equipment, cooking equipment, sinks, pantry equipment, working tables, and utensils.

47

The tables and chairs, if a comfortable, good quality chair is used, can also be budgeted at about $50.00 per seat; for 160 seats the cost will be about $8,000. If special furniture is required, this figure probably should be supplemented to take that into consideration, suggesting a budget item of $16,000 for tables, chairs, and associated furniture.

This leaves $579,000 to buy the land and to build the building.

The grading and completion of a parking lot for fifty cars, for example, will cost about $2,000 per car space. This figure is difficult to establish and should be verified by estimates from local grading contractors since it can range according to jurisdiction and soil conditions, anywhere from $1,000 to $3,000 per space. However, for the purposes of illustration, let us budget land improvement at $100,000.

There is now a balance of $479,000 for purchase of land and for construction of a building.

One of the critical factors affecting the entire formula usually is the availability of an appropriate site at a cost that is compatible with the overall investment. Actually one of the most important considerations affecting the success of your venture will be the selection of the site; and this is not an area in which one should attempt to economize.

The building itself will have to be budgeted by the designer, taking into consideration that the combined cost of the site and the building should not exceed $479,000.

If a prime site is available for $150,000 this would provide $329,000 to construct a building of about 6000 sq. ft.

Your designer, then, would be working to design a building to be constructed according to the building codes that, including decorative treatment, signs, lighting, and all other elements, would cost about $50.00 to $60.00 per sq. ft.

48

### Budget Benders

We are assuming that $6,000 or $10,000 would be required for expendable items such as silverware, dishes, china, table-cloths, napkins, and menus.

This leaves about $19,000 for advertising for preopening promotion, hiring personnel, and other miscellaneous items or adjustments.

To accomplish such a design under today's cost parameters and remain within a $50 to $60 per sq. ft. budget figure will require a skilled and knowledgeable approach to the design problem and the effective integration of space within the building, together with simple exterior lines.

In the design for this building you will want to avoid roof sections, such as dormers and gables, beyond those absolutely necessary to accomplish your design result.

You will want to minimize ceiling spans since the larger span a beam must carry, the more costly the beam per foot of length, and the earlier the transition to steel is necessary. Steel is even more costly than wood, not only in terms of material costs but in terms of the cost of skills required to put it in place.

It would appear then that the design of a building meeting the requirements set forth here would be for a conventionally constructed frame and/or brick veneer building, containing two or three smaller dining rooms and a kitchen area built around an appropriate flow diagram of the operation.

In the event that your site is situated in an area where there is little competition and a great need for restaurant service, a conservative estimate of annual sales might well be higher than the example used in this illustration and, based upon such a carefully arrived at judgment, might lead to the conclusion that you can afford to put more money into either your building or land cost.

49

The major pitfall is that as you begin planning, your enthusiasm and interest gain momentum, while your propensity for objectivity will fade. You will tend to rationalize, or ignore sticky points that do not fall into place nicely. If it is necessary to dream a bit to hype your projected sales figures in order to justify a little extra building cost, you will try to do so. Don't feel badly about the temptation. So-called sophisticated sales people sometimes begin with the bottom line, and work backwards to justify selling a particular account.

On the other hand, don't be surprised when this liberty with facts comes back to haunt you as you try to support that extra $50,000 or $100,000 that you rationalized into the operation early on. If you take a cavalier approach to your early computations, you will have to pay the piper.

# Designing
# Your
# Facility

# 7

As has been previously discussed, the designing of this facility should not be turned over to an architect until the appropriate site surveys, demographic and psychographic studies have been completed, and design criteria have been established relative to exterior image and interior flow of materials. This interior flow will be built around such factors as the type of menu and cooking operation which you will have.

When you get into the specific phase of coordinating with an architect or engineer on a specific building design, there are numerous considerations that can make a great deal of difference in initial cost, eventual maintenance cost, and the end result generally.

If your site has been carefully selected, there will be no unusual underground or topographic problems and you will be building approximately on grade.

In today's (1981) market the cost of filling a restaurant site, suitable for a family sit-down restaurant in a suburban location, approximately one foot (in other words, raising the level of grade one foot) will average in the area of $15,000.

It should be obvious, then, in planning your construction that if you choose a site that will require a significant raising of grade or elevation that you can very quickly add $20,000, $40,000, or $60,000 without realizing it.

## Earthwork

The earthwork that must be done will have to cover cutting of roadways for driveways, the parking lot, and filling with an appropriate fill to give sufficient compaction to support paving, landscaping, curbing, and so forth.

In your contract, or in specifications to your general contractor and the subcontractor concerned with this work, you will want to make it clear that all public streets and roadways will be protected and kept free of obstructions, and that trees and shrubs will be protected from damage to the fullest extent possible.

It is usually desirable to put the roadbed for driveways in very early in the job and require that all trucks delivering material to the job stay on these roadways.

This precaution generally avoids bumping and barking trees and cutting up the rest of the area with heavy truck tires so that after a little bit of rain you end up with a real mess on your hands.

Incidentally, when you end up with a mess on your hands, you can assume that it is going to cost you more money to get the job done.

The contractor should also be required throughout the job to protect his excavation; this means providing trenches to prevent water damage that during certain times of the year can be a very serious problem.

Generally, a clean construction job is an efficient construction job; and when one gets some experience, he can assess the professionalism of the contractor just by walking through the work area for a short period of time. It is desirable to insist that the contractor clean up all accumulated debris and rubbish every day during construction and remove the accumulation from the building and surrounding premises.

Cleaning up the area might appear at first to represent extra effort, but it has been proven time and time again that the contractor's employees work much more efficiently without a lot of debris under foot, that the job will actually go better, and that the finished work will reflect a higher professional standard. Besides, a neat area makes a good impression on the public.

If winter weather becomes a factor because you're beginning construction either in early spring or late autumn, specific attention should be given to ensuring that the contractor protect all of his work from freezing temperatures during the construction until a permanent heating system is ready for use.

The construction can be protected by means such as vented salamanders or temporary boilers with canvas enclosures. Maintaining temperatures of about 50° in the working areas is not really difficult except in the most bitter cold with high winds.

In the event that salamanders are used, however, there is a caution with respect to proper smoke pipes or venting in order to avoid safety hazards.

In the earthwork portion of the job will be included all earthwork for the building, covering the excavation and backfilling for footings and foundations, piers, walls, platforms as well as the porous or aggregate fill under all concrete slab and the disposal of excess excavated material from the site when necessary, and the clean-up of the area after completion of the earthwork.

Normally, a plan is established at the outset that provides for stripping and stockpiling topsoil in order that the topsoil may be used later for rough, or, when of sufficient quality, finished grading. Whenever excavations are made for walls, such as foundation walls, the excavations should be at least 1½ to 2 feet wider than the wall in order to provide a sufficient amount of clearance for working with forms and to prevent sliding or caving banks.

In sandy soil, the excavations might have to be considerably wider in order to accomplish the same purpose.

Oftentimes if proper grades are taken, excess filling can be "lost" or used up on the site, avoiding the extra cost of carting it away.

However, whenever filling or backfilling, the fill material should be kept free from frost, roots, and debris; and this material should be backfilled in layers, not filling more than eight or ten inches at a time in order to provide for proper compaction, that is compressing of the soil.

This procedure will avoid damage that might be caused later by additional settling that results in the cracking of hard surfaces.


## Concrete Slab

Usually when concrete slabs are going to be placed on grade—and, incidentally, this is the least expensive way of constructing a building—soil, under normal circumstances, should be removed for a minimum of one foot below the grade. If unusual soil conditions exist, an engineer's advice should be sought as to whether or not it is desirable to go to a lower depth.

54

The excavated area then should be filled with selected materials placed in layers and compacted to 95 percent compaction by test before the concrete is actually poured.

Normally, information as to specifications and standards for testing of concrete work can be obtained from the American Society of Testing Materials or from the American Concrete Institute in their booklet, *Building Code Requirements for Reinforced Concrete.* Both organizations provide excellent guidelines for working with concrete.

A detailed specification will be established for the mixture to be used in preparing the cement, such as American Society of Testing Materials Standard 150, using Portland Cement plus a specification for the gravel or sand to be used in the mix, the latter designated by sieve sizes.

Steel bar and mesh reinforcing materials are also specified by the American Society of Testing Materials. A superior job can be obtained by using a surface hardener and dustproofing compound, particularly on floor surfaces.

Actually, a hard surface concrete floor, using a surface hardener and dustproofing compound, such as those manufactured by companies like Armortop of Anti-Hydro and Kemi-Kote of Tremco Manufacturing Company, produces, in effect, the same results for all practical purposes as a quarry tile in the kitchen areas and at a considerably lower cost.

Whenever slabs are placed on the ground, of course, a vapor barrier should be used, usually a polyethylene film.

Your architect will probably want to take samples from each pouring of concrete. These will be used to certify that the proper cure for the concrete has been used.

Normally, the architect or engineer will take about six samples from each pour and will break open two after three days for examination. The next two samples will be broken open at seven days and the last two at about a month. On a major building, a load or compression test will also be done on the cored sample to verify test results for areas where the loads are going to be placed in the structure.

It is desirable to do trimming and refilling close to poured concrete walls by hand, rather than with heavy equipment in order to get a cleaner job and to avoid unnecessary, inadvertent damage to construction.

While it is common practice today to pour concrete year-round, it is really undesirable to do so at temperatures lower than 40°F. Only when absolutely necessary should concrete be poured below this temperature.

If cold-weather pouring is unavoidable, the contractor should be required to provide equipment for heating and protecting concrete during near-freezing weather and no materials containing ice or frost should be used. The temperature of the concrete poured should be maintained above 50°F. for not less than five days after placing it—and in the case of thin slabs, at least one week.

The housing or other protection used to cover the concrete should be left in place at least a day after the heat has been eliminated. The use of salt, calcium chloride, or other materials in concrete mixtures to prevent freezing, while widespread, is not really a desirable practice.

People express a great deal of concern about the problem of concrete handling in cold weather, but few realize that there is a problem also in handling concrete during warm weather. During such weather conditions, special care and precautions have to be taken to prevent premature drying.

In using a hard surface concrete floor, either without adding quarry tile or as a finished floor, concrete should be smoothed by a process called "floating" while the concrete is still green although hardened sufficiently to bear the worker's weight. A metal, disc power machine should be used. The machine is carefully controlled in its operation to prevent overworking the finish and drawing excess water to the surface, so that the resulting surface has almost a glass-like finish.

## Main Building Structure

Assuming that your restaurant building is average in size, its main structure will normally fall into one of three categories. It will be constructed with either a wood frame, traditional and quite commonly seen; or, as has been more prevalent in recent years, of structural steel; or masonry.

Each of these methods of construction provides advantages and disadvantages.

### Wood Frame

Wood frame is a type of construction readily handled by practically all contractors and carpenters and, therefore, one can be fairly certain of satisfactory accomplishment.

On the other hand, most building codes begin to impose rather serious restrictions upon wood frame or other combustible construction when a building begins to approach 4,000 to 5,000 sq. ft. in total floor area.

It can, therefore, be worth your while to check the building codes in your particular area when you begin to consider constructing a restaurant facility to accommodate more than 150 seats or so. At that point you will be approaching the dividing line where many of the fire code considerations apply and the additional fire protection standards that will have to be included in your construction could well offset the advantages of simplicity and ease of the wood frame construction.

### Structural Steel

Structural steel is now available in a form that parallels wood construction in that steel beams, studs, and trusses are now made that accept nails.

57

This type of steel material is normally cut and drilled in the shop, avoiding the necessity for any burning of holes on the job.

The use of Penmetal and other similar materials, however, also presents a requirement for a degree of expertise not so prevalent among smaller contractors. When using Penmetal, an additional trade is involved: steel workers. There are also some special considerations such as the use of cables and turnbuckles to avoid wind damage and racking. The Steel Joist Institute puts out an excellent publication, *Standard Specifications for Open Web Steel Joist Construction and Long Span Series,* which is worthy of reference in this regard.

*Light Metal Framing*   Light metal framing is designed and produced by companies such as Penmetal Structural Company, Strand-Steel Corporation, or J. K. Parker, Inc. (Parko steel sections) to mention a few.

These companies produce sheet steel or strips and light metal steel studs that are nailable as well as structural steel shapes. The steel has to be fireproofed.

Contractors who are familiar with light metal framing will find it no problem whatever; however, contractors who have not had experience with this method of construction could get themselves into problems by going ahead without qualified supervision and direction.

### Masonry

Masonry construction takes many forms but basically will be a cement block, cinder block, or brick building construction. From the point of view of this author, taking all things into consideration, it is probably the preferred method of construction for a building between 5,000 and 10,000 sq. ft. in size.

Buildings of smaller size than 5,000 sq. ft. are quite satisfactory when of wood frame construction while there is great

58

advantage in the use of structural steel construction for larger buildings.

*Prefabricated.*　In some locations and situations, the building problem can well be addressed by utilization of a prefabricated building, for example, a "Butler building," or similar type. When working with a prefabricated structure, one must take great care to give the face, or front of the building its special character of appearance. It's important to be very careful to avoid ending up with a building that does not have a "foodservice identity" or with one that blends into the surroundings in a manner that permits potential customers to pass by without being aware of the nature of the business contained in the building.

Signs can help give a restaurant its identity, but they are only a partial answer. In some cases a mural or other treatment on the sides of the building will be needed to do the trick. While the prefabricated steel building or its counterpart is a legitimate course, it is one that must be carefully handled.

Another excellent course of action for the entrepreneur is that of occupying suitable space in or near the entrance of a well-traveled shopping mall. Here, a location that assures high visibility in a high traffic location is vital. When utilizing this course, one must be sure to ascertain the degree to which hours of operation of the shopping mall will be a factor and to find out whether or not the restaurant can be located in such a manner as to be open at times when the shopping mall itself is closed to the public.

## Roofs

There are several types of roofing. Among them is the so-called built-up roofing which is a series of layers of asphalt felt and gravel, usually on a flat or almost flat roof. There are also

59

asbestos strip shingles and, of course, various types of tiles, slates, and wood shakes.

The selection of roof material will be determined by two fundamental considerations:

1.  The desirability of a flat roof over your kitchen area, particularly if it is out of the general view of the public. This facilitates putting air compressors and vents on the roof instead of through the sides of the building.

The obvious advantage of putting these on the roof is that duct runs are much shorter, and consequently, the impellor units and other equipment can be of lower power requirement. In addition, the exhaust nuisance is up over a flat roof, and, therefore, less noticeable and offensive in the parking lot and surrounding area.

It is surprising how seldom this method is considered since it is a highly efficient approach to this area of construction, having significant cost advantages as well as offering aesthetic advantages.

2.  Your choice of materials for the roof of the main building will be determined primarily by aesthetics; however, comparable aesthetic results can be achieved through the use of a wide range of products.

For example, either a slate or a shake roof of an average roof area and pitch, covering 5,000 sq. ft. of floor, cost about $20,000 to $28,000 to put in place in 1979.

However, a similar result can be obtained for about half that amount of money by using some of the concrete roof tiles, such as Doric, or by using a heavy-duty, strip shingle.

Strip shingles, I am happy to say, now come in substantial thicknesses with various design cuts. This feature makes them a very desirable and relatively inexpensive roof material both from a cost point of view and a practical point of view, except in those instances when design requirements indicate slate or other materials to achieve authenticity.

Where authenticity is a factor, however, you will not be as concerned with budgetary factors as you are with aesthetic factors. In this book, however, we are attempting to give the reader some indications as to which means he might use to accomplish his end result without incurring unnecessary or excessive costs.

It is amazing to see the number of buildings that are constructed without a good job of caulking. You should insist that all joints—those between masonry and frames, windows and the basic wall frames, between masonry and steel, between wood battens and stucco, between main walls and caps or flashings, in fact, all joints in general—be properly caulked.

Caulking is best done by using oakum, a dry spun, rope-like material and caulking compound (a manufactured compound developed for this purpose).

In general, caulking is done with a caulking gun that forces compound through a nozzle with sufficient pressure to fill these crevices properly. Caulking will go a long way toward creating a tight building and a comfortable building, preventing such difficulties as air leaks and drafts when the building is later occupied.

## Carpentry

In discussing a wood building, we often hear people preoccupied with using kiln-dried lumber in a building that will have a plaster finish.

It is our feeling that this is somewhat naive in that when the wet plaster goes on the wall, tons of water are put into the building. The kiln-dried dimension then becomes somewhat academic.

You should have, however, lumber that is straight, reasonably seasoned, and free of knots for your rough lumber.

When it comes to finished lumber or decorator's materials, it will be worth your while to look at a number of polyurethane and other plastic materials on the market that simulate rough-hewn beams, wall paneling, and other decorative features.

This material is excellently produced and if cleverly used, can simplify the process of providing a beamed ceiling, since the polyurethane beam would merely be cemented to the ceiling. In some instances such a beam can also be used as a conduit for electrical cables or other similar runs.

Whenever a so-called dry wall finish is used in lieu of plaster, this should really be constructed with a double-layer system with the first layer nailed or stapled to the studs and the second layer applied to the first layer by cement or adhesive. The joints on the face layer should not coincide with the joints on the sheet behind; and the joints should be taped, plastered and sanded in the usual fashion.

This type of dry-wall construction, in this author's opinion, is really superior to plaster; however, we would surely get a great deal of debate on this point from the trades.

## Plaster

Whenever plaster is going to be used, it should never be applied at temperatures below freezing. A minimum temperature of around 50° to 60°F. should be maintained for a period after the application of the plaster until the plaster is completely dry.

In no case should plaster be subjected to low temperatures; in cold, damp weather properly regulated heat has to be provided in the plastered area.

It is also true that in hot, dry weather too-rapid drying has to be avoided, another factor which is usually not considered by those using plaster construction.

## Finishing

### Exterior Finish

Stucco exterior finishes are usually applied in three coats; don't let the contractor talk you into a one-coat job. These coats will normally be (1) a base coat, called a scratch coat, covered by (2) a brown coat that should not be applied to the wall sooner than forty-eight hours after the scratch coat has been put on, and, (3) the finish coat that carries the color and texture you desire for your finish.

### Floor Finish

A great deal can be accomplished in terms of aesthetics and decor by the use of tile and other floor coverings. Many entrepreneurs are now taking the position that carpeting costs no more than the various types of asbestos or other manufactured tiles, presents a more attractive finish, and is less costly to maintain.

With the exception of the kitchen area, you can feel well advised in any event to use carpeting throughout, if it is available at comparable or lower cost than other floor materials. This probably will be surprising to you, but a check on costs will verify that it is true.

### Wall Coverings and Wall Finishings

An area where you have wide latitude of choice is in wall coverings and finishings. These go all the way from conventional materials to wallpapers of various qualities and grades. You may also wish to consider vinyl wall covering, such as Vicrotex, which not only provides you with a decorative finish but has a fire-retardant rating.

There are one or two companies coming into the business now who will design and manufacture a completely prefabricated and finished interior for restaurants and other buildings, delivering it to the job when the building has reached that stage of construction. This type of service makes it possible to install your interior finish in a remarkably short time. We have seen restaurant interiors installed in less than one week using this method.

Incidentally, this method is particularly desirable in remodeling or repair jobs that involve repairing substantial damage from causes such as water or fire.

## Legal Ordinances and Codes

Of course, in every instance it is extremely desirable to contact your local building inspector, fire inspector, and health inspector early in the planning stages. You will find that these officials will be very pleased that you thought to contact them for their advice early in the game; and you will find that long experience in their respective jurisdictions can be very helpful to you in avoiding problems later and in simplifying your problems of meeting code requirements.

While in the past building inspectors have tended to be extremely rigid in terms of permitting new methods and materials, happily the trend is now toward much more leniency in this area. Today, there is far greater latitude to work with a

64

wider range of new materials and techniques, a long overdue development.

In some cases material selection can impact very favorably upon fire insurance and liability rates, as well as upon initial cost of construction. Real payoffs in reduced overhead can be realized too, particularly in the area of ever-increasing costs of utilities. Good insulation, proper ventilation of compressors in order to dissipate heat in hot weather, and the installation of mist-generating units which reduce the cost of air conditioning are only a few of the energy-saving measures you can take.

Proper treatment of air conditioning installations can easily reduce monthly electric bills by as much as 40 or 50 percent. Tinted glass windows, appropriately designed overhangs, and similar treatments of design can generate even greater savings.

These energy-saving devices are very important when one remembers that in today's operating environment your single largest uncontrollable expense, once the building is built, will be electricity. Extra attention in this area will pay big dividends over time, for it is obvious that the days of cheap power are forever gone.

# Kitchen Design

**8**

Historically, the design of restaurant kitchens has been a cumbersome process, resulting too often in more equipment than necessary to do an effective job.

Kitchen designers have been essentially copiers of prior designs by architects who are actually "packaging engineers", as opposed to "industrial engineers" versed in the science of time and motion and knowledgeable about the flow of materials.

A kitchen is essentially a production facility for the purpose of efficiently transforming raw materials into finished and assembled meals ready for delivery to the customer's table.

To properly design such a facility, one must be conversant with the elements of production as well as the steps involved and the skills required to accomplish the production goals. To ascertain from the equipment manufacturer those combinations of equipment which in his opinion constitute the various packages necessary for a pantry, for a cooking area, for a salad area, and for a dishwashing area, too often results in an over-equipped facility, hence an unnecessarily costly facility.

Not only is this extra cost traceable to the purchase of excessive equipment and capacity, but there are also cost penalties for excessive floor area (which add up impressively at a rate of $50.00 to $90.00 per foot) and cost penalties for additional electrical wiring, drainage lines, water lines, and so forth.

Furthermore, the continuing cost of higher utility bills and the labor required to man an overbuilt facility impose a penalty upon the operation that makes it necessary for that operation to generate higher sales than originally anticipated in order to reach a point of turning a profit, which after all is the objective.

The most significant new ingredient involved in the design of kitchens is that of energy transfer and utilization. There are numerous sources of heat in a restaurant. For example, compressors, motors, ranges, and ovens; and in the past the heat generated by these sources has been handled through the application of air conditioning.

The largest single fixed expense is the cost of utilities and this cost is essentially uncontrollable. Hence, engineering effort that is addressed to the idea of capturing, filtering, and redistributing the heat generated by utilities will pay big dividends, especially in cold climates. Also, consideration given to containing heat, immediately dissipating it, or reducing it in other ways will greatly reduce your energy costs.

Because of new energy-saving requirements, the type of construction used in the last few years for franchise or chain operations will soon become a thing of the past. Passive systems of energy conservation and redistribution, engineered

68

into new construction, will be necessary in the future. Use of solar panels to produce hot water requirements is also worthy of serious consideration when designing a restaurant.

The minor reduction in energy utilization in one of the typical "glass block with a roof on top" buildings can quickly amount to a couple hundred dollars each month per location. Given 200, 300, 400 or more locations, this savings means the transfer of a million or more dollars, immediately and simply, to the bottom line. Alert managements will become increasingly aware of and interested in this dimension, as the energy crisis continues and the availability of inexpensive energy becomes forever a thing of the past.

## Advances in Equipment Design

Of course, the menu that you have set up will have more bearing than does any other factor on your kitchen layout; however, it is noteworthy that in recent years some rather spectacular advances in the area of kitchen equipment have taken place.

Many manufacturers have developed microwave units, infrared units, pressure-cooking equipment, and other devices designed to expedite the flow of food preparation through a kitchen.

One of the more exciting and unusual devices to come on the market in recent years is the Foster Recon unit which uses a combination of infrared and convection heat and which in tests has shown itself to perform the tasks of several pieces of kitchen equipment including the broiler, the griddle and the oven.

When looking at equipment, do not overlook items like Mist-Mizer, a device which when added to air conditioner units can result in a marked reduction of energy consumption and therefore in substantial savings. Automatic and timed thermostats are also worthy of special thought in conjunction with your equipment considerations.

## Layout for Kitchen

Figure A, following, is a kitchen layout produced for an installation requiring preparation facilities to service a sit-down counter as well as a dining room with about 140 seats. It will be noted that the design strives to be practical in terms of providing equipment that will, with a minimum of labor, support a counter service, luncheon menu, breakfast menu, and dinner menu.

The preparation table has been designed to put everything at the fingertips of the chef, who works behind it and can service the counter through a pass-through at point (8). All of the preparation is built around the chef in items identified by (17), (18), (13), (14), (15), (16), (20), (21), (22), and (23). The equipment is positioned so as to require the cook to move only a step or two in any direction to tie everything together; yet it is laid out in such a way as to enable two cooks to work efficiently side by side in the crush of a maximum production load.

This layout is further supplemented by an efficient traffic flow for service personnel, which not only provides for expediting service, but also for the supplemental effort of service personnel in preparing set ups, adding condiments, and performing similar tasks.

The flow of materials from receiving into and through the preparation process is continuous and orderly, as is the flow of dishes from the preparation area to the dining room, then back through dishwashing and returning to the preparation area.

The use of self-leveling dispensers provides for maximum storage of dishes, heated and at hand for the make up of plates.

70

While it is not suggested that this method is the only way in which an efficient kitchen area can be accomplished, the design does illustrate the practicability of a minimum-cost layout to service a comprehensive menu offering, with all equipment being adequately spaced within an area having a ratio of about 20 percent preparation area to 80 percent dining area, as opposed to the conventional 45 percent preparation to 55 percent dining usually found in such installations.

This facility occupies approximately 400 square feet of space, yet provides everything necessary to get the job done, without undue reliance upon personnel or overburdening of personnel.

## Analyze What's New

Recent breakthroughs in equipment design have resulted in multipurpose equipment that can handle alone jobs that once required several pieces of equipment, with consequent reduction in space and manpower requirements and without any disadvantage insofar as quality is concerned.

Actually, some of these equipment items bring to the preparation area some very significant advantages: more uniform results, lesser levels of skill required to accomplish the preparation task, a faster rate of production, less shrinkage, and similar benefits.

A fine piece of equipment, not utilized in this particular layout but of inestimable value as an expediter in certain types of operations, is the microwave, originally developed by Raytheon Corporation and later marketed by a number of companies in a variety of models and sizes.

This equipment has met with considerable resistance, partly because of ineptness in its original marketing approach, and also because of the zeal of manufacturers to sell it as a do-all, rather than to concentrate upon its real advantages and

71

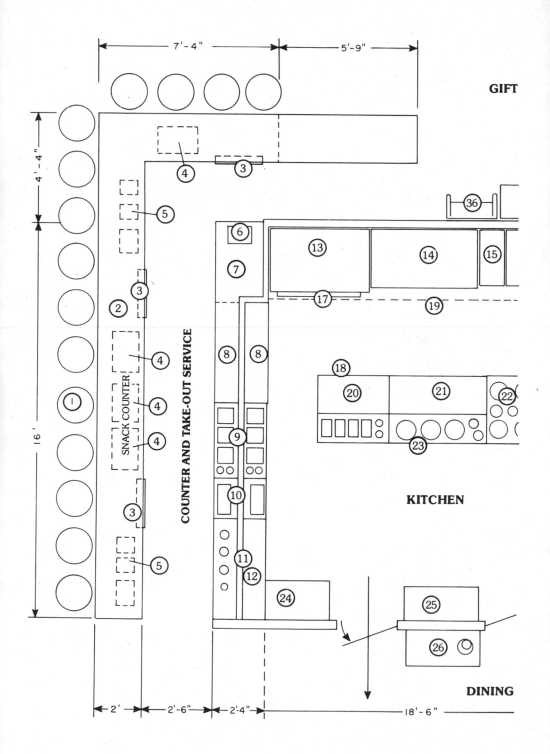

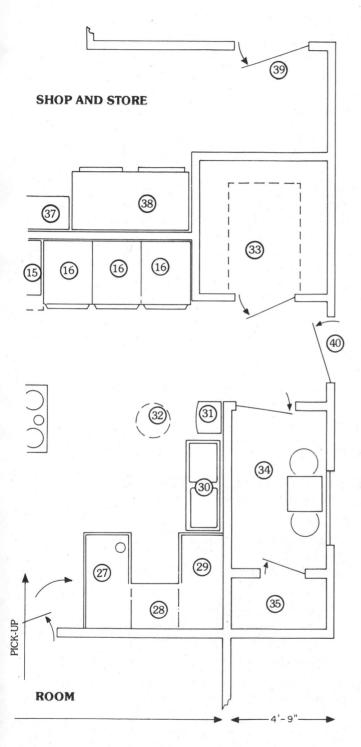

**SHOP AND STORE**

**ROOM**

PICK-UP

4'-9"

| | ITEM |
|---|---|
| **1** | Stools (15) |
| **2** | Formica Counter |
| **3** | Silver Racks |
| **4** | Soiled Dish Tote Boxes |
| **5** | Glasses, Mats, Napkins |
| **6** | Cash Register |
| **7** | Merchandise Display |
| **8** | Pass Thru Shelf |
| **9** | Ice Cream Cabinets |
| **10** | Ice Bin — Two Sided |
| **11** | Soft Drink Hds. + Water |
| **12** | $CO_2$ & Syrup (Under) |
| **13** | Foster Recon |
| **14** | Range W/Griddle Top |
| **15** | Fryers |
| **16** | 3 Sec. Refr.(2)/Freezer(1) |
| **17** | Refr. Under |
| **18** | Refr. Under |
| **19** | Exhaust Hood |
| **20** | Sandwich Unit |
| **21** | Prep & Steam Tables |
| **22** | Plates — Lowerators |
| **23** | Serving Shelf |
| **24** | Coffee Maker — Cups |
| **25** | Display — Desserts |
| **26** | Setups — Mats, Water, Napkins. Glasses |
| **27** | Soiled Dish Table |
| **28** | Washer |
| **29** | Landing |
| **30** | 2 Hole Sink |
| **31** | Hand Sink |
| **32** | Exhaust Fan |
| **33** | Dry Storage |
| **34** | Dressing Room |
| **35** | Closet |
| **36** | Pay Telephone |
| **37** | Cigarette Machine |
| **38** | Store Refr. Display |
| **39** | Relocated Door |
| **40** | Receiving |
| SCALE: ¼" = 1' | |
| D. A. DYER | |

73

to market it on a basis of understanding of what happens in a food operation.

It is not our purpose to endorse any individual equipment or manufacturer but rather through documented results to emphasize the point that one should not arbitrarily turn his back upon new innovations in the equipment field. If an operator does this, he foolishly precludes the opportunity to avail himself of advances in technology through a blind adherence to tradition, based primarily on the uneasiness and lack of confidence expressed by his technicians (food preparation personnel) which, in turn, rises out of their lack of confidence, or unwillingness to try something new.

We do not by any means suggest that you should become the testing laboratory for every manufacturer with a new idea. Rather, we suggest a searching evaluation of equipment advances against your specific requirements, based upon objective analysis, free from prejudice or arbitrary resistance to change.

## Dishwashing Facility

One area of potentially great cost, and usually of considerable confusion, is the provision of a dishwashing facility.

In our opinion, the best dishwashing facility is a three-hole sink with an employee dishwasher. However, it becomes increasingly difficult to hire dishwashers on a dependable basis and many restaurant owners feel that they want to have an automatic dishwashing facility.

In our opinion, after having done many time and motion studies, the smallest, three-stage dishwashing machine made by any principal manufacturer, such as Hobart or Blakeslee, is more than adequate for a restaurant with up to 200 seats.

This type of machine will adequately handle the flow generated by 200 people at a peak operation, provided it is installed in such a way as to provide a landing area for scrapping, with a lead-in tray or counter of sufficient capacity to stack up five or six racks ahead of the machine, and a landing area at the exhaust end of the machine capable of holding five or six additional racks for the purpose of air-drying.

The time taken for a load to pass through the machine itself, the actual dishwashing time, is the shortest segment in the entire process of scrapping and washing. Thus, the basis of a dishwashing facility must be consideration of the total operation in terms of time and motion, beginning with the landing of the dishes, the scrapping of the dishes, the racking, the processing of the racks through the machine, the stacking of the racks for air-drying, and the eventual return of the dishes to dish carts or shelves or other appropriate storage.

A person employed as a dishwasher normally will scrap and rack until he gets one, two or three racks ahead and then begin processing them through the machine. He will concentrate on the scrapping and racking because once the racks go into the machine, they will move out much faster than he can feed the machine.

When he gets a moment in this sequence, as the flow of dishes into the kitchen fluctuates, he will then remove the air-dried dishes from the storage area at the exhaust end of the machine and return them to their appropriate storage place.

The dishwashing operation in a restaurant of 150 to 200 seats can be handled quite adequately by one person.

In the event that you really are not convinced of this, you can always consider having a porter or busboy assist if necessary for a half hour or so during the peak of your day's operation.

## Consultant's Report

The following is a typical preliminary report of a consulting effort involving examination of a transient facility with multifaceted operation including foodservice, snack bar, service station, gift shop, and other areas. (See Figure A on pages 72 and 73.) The objective here was to provide a practical compromise in the food preparation facility without expanding the size of the building or robbing the customer areas in order to gain kitchen space.

The approach and rationale will be of assistance to individuals examining their own facilities, since it provides a fabric of logic on which to structure such an examination.

***

**From:**  Consultant

**To:**  Customer

**Subject:**  Special study, food preparation facility

OBJECTIVE: The objective of this assignment is (1) to review the present facilities; (2) to make recommendations as appropriate to provide for a preparation facility capable of meeting maximum reasonable anticipated demands upon it, yet capable of expanding and contracting in its manpower requirements as the season and demand varies; (3) to attempt to obtain the desired result with a minimum of expansion requirements on the building.

ASSUMPTIONS: In seeking the objectives, certain planning assumptions, which were discussed with management, were established. These were essentially that customers tend to fall into three general categories: (a) customers residing on premises; (b) transients such as gasoline customers; (c) local area residents who come to know and enjoy the facility.

The requirement to service these different categories of customers places certain conflicting requirements upon

76

the foodservice facility and makes it advisable to provide food service during a long operating day.

Breakfast service must embrace some time frame such as 7:00 A.M. to 9:00 A.M. During this period the main load on the kitchen is for such items as eggs, cooked to order; breakfast meats including bacon, sausage links, and ham; toast or biscuits.

EQUIPMENT PROVIDED: Included is a griddle or range top adequate for egg production plus an oven where biscuits, either baking soda or brown and serve, can be heated under the Foster unit. Toasters can be placed on coffee pick-up station also. Breakfast meats can be produced in any variety and amounts, quickly and well done in the Foster Recon unit.

Transients in the period between 9:00 A.M. and 11:00 A.M. will, for the most part, be interested in coffee, pastries, toast, or other light snacks, all of which pose no special problems.

Luncheon trade will no doubt fall between 11:00 or 11:30 A.M. and 3:30 P.M. During this period the principal demand will be for steak specials, hamburgers, hamburger plates, cheeseburgers, and various other specials. Seventy percent of the demand will be for beef items. THE PRIMARY EQUIPMENT FOR THIS SERVICE IS: (a) griddle and Foster Recon, which will take food item-by-item on a cook-to-order basis and rapidly turn out a delightful product. French fries can be cooked to order in the fryers, as with fried shrimp platters. It is recommended that fried chicken, which otherwise will be a troublesome item, be cooked ahead and refrigerated, then reconstituted in the Foster Recon on an order basis. This procedure will give you an exceptional result and can relieve pressure on the kitchen by allowing the cook to prepare ahead during the mid-morning slack period.

The afternoon period from 3:30 or 4:00 to 4:30 P.M. or so will be quite light. This less hectic time will enable you to set up a two-shift operation, with a counter attendant handling demands during that 2½ hour period.

Dinner will no doubt begin around 6:40 or 7:00 in the evening and build into the 9:00 to 10:30 P.M. time frame. Here you will have a demand for the full range of menu items, and again the cook-to-order ability of the Foster Recon will enable you to handle this peak, particularly if some advance preparation is done. For example, chicken can be partially cooked, and hamburger patties can be made ahead of time.

From about 11:00 P.M. on, the service should be tapered back to a hot-sandwich, and snack-service, providing time for the daily cleanup and tally of usage as a basis for ordering replacements.

The morning slack period is a good time for the cook to do his ordering, and the facility provides ample storage for accepting deliveries of perishables only twice a week, probably Monday and Friday.

A very efficient traffic pattern is established for waiters and waitresses, with the ability to drop dishes off on a soiled dish table when coming into the kitchen and either pick up or assemble and pick up on the way out of the kitchen.

It is suggested that pickup for soft drinks such as cola and root beer be at the counter side where the soft drink beverage station is situated, thereby enabling this station

78

to handle both the dining room and the snack bar with little problem.

We have not provided for a milk dispenser since we feel that this is an unnecessary expenditure and utilization of space, since the store now stocks milk for campers, and it is easy to place a few cartons for the occasional call in the set-up area. This will also enable you to make available a choice of white, chocolate, and strawberry flavored milk.

You might also consider specials from time to time in the beef pot pie beef stew categories, and we would strongly recommend that you add spaghetti to your regular menu.

MISCELLANEOUS DATA: You will also note that rubberoid or plastic tote boxes are situated on shelves under the snack counter so that soiled dishes may be accumulated to be carried back to the dishwashing area when convenient. Racks for silverware and storage of place mats, napkins, etc., and other items also conveniently situated here.

The relationship of all elements of service is such as to minimize lost motion and to maximize speed of service during peak periods. Slack periods can be used for cleanup and restocking.

POSSIBLE FUTURE CONSULTING AREAS: As you progress with this program, you may wish later to obtain additional consulting assistance in the assembly of a purchasing, inventory control, foodservice record-keeping system, which can be quite simply assembled, making it possible for the cook to do essentially all of the basic accounting for the foodservice and to maintain proper review of food costs and other expenses.

You may also desire assistance in the area of identifying and relating convenience foods presently on the market to your foodservice needs in order to develop further uniformity and control as well as to avoid the necessity for highly trained kitchen personnel in areas where they may be unavailable or inordinately expensive to hire for this kind of operation.

Please note that the above excerpts from an actual consulting report illustrate the logical flow of elements of consideration in planning a food preparation facility. First, the objective is stated. Secondly, planning assumptions are stated, thereby framing the problem to be solved.

Next, an actual design is worked around a flow diagram illustrating the flow of materials, and relating the pressures upon the facility to serving hours, type of service required, and other elements. Finally, follow-on planning areas are identified to create an ongoing continuity.

This report is an excellent example of a situation where new equipment on the market was ideally suited to filling a specific need and, in the opinion of the consultant, could do so better than alternative choices.

# Staffing and the Manager

# 9

Unlike most other businesses, a restaurant is at least a six-day and often a seven-day-a-week affair; and its peak hours of business are evening hours, weekends, and holidays, periods of time that are normally leisure hours for other people.

There are those who go into the restaurant business with the idea that it will be a pleasant form of retirement and find, after having done so, that they are working twice as hard and twice as long as they ever did in the past. On the other hand, and particularly in these days, there are investors who do not consider the restaurant business to require any effort beyond cooking food, serving it to customers, and taking their money.

As a matter of fact, there is probably no business that requires more in terms of logistics, planning, or effective coordination of staff, and yet where these aspects are more taken for granted.

In the investor-owned restaurant, oftentimes the owner, who does not understand the business, has only one solution to operating problems: fire the manager.

A common practice among owner managers is not to provide sufficient relief help so they themselves can lead normal lives and spend an appropriate portion of their time with their families.

## In-Depth Organization

Although no two restaurants will be exactly alike, there are certain principles that will apply pretty much to all restaurants. The manager, above all, should be a people-oriented, team-oriented individual. Too often the manager, in an effort to make himself a key man, attempts to set things up so that only he can make decisions. This is bad organization, even in the smallest restaurant. It is obvious that such a manager either becomes a prisoner on the premises or, in the event of an emergency during his absence, none of the other employees wants to, or feels as though he should, make an appropriate decision. Every business organization, and particularly a restaurant, should be organized "in depth."

In most restaurant locations there will be many people, such as students, teachers, homemakers, and others, who will welcome an opportunity to make extra dollars on a part-time or on a call basis.

These people represent good, intelligent personnel and, if a proper training program is provided to train them for the work and orient them to the job, many of the positions in the restaurant can be very adequately handled by such personnel.

82

This point, of course, brings up the question of proper organization and training, the lack of which can have a disastrous impact upon the restaurant operation. Running a restaurant without advance preparation and training of personnel should be regarded as seriously as operating the restaurant without proper insurance or sufficient daily food supply.

Most restaurants will be organized into one or two shifts, depending upon whether luncheon is served, or only dinner. It is impractical for one manager to supervise the operation for sixteen or seventeen hours each day and therefore the necessity for an in-depth organization becomes even more apparent.

## Whole Day Schedule

The hours during which the restaurant operates will be divided into two types of activity. There will be that period of time before opening in which food is being received and prepared, and the various chores are being completed, and on completion of the work day, the time during which cleanup and similar chores should be accomplished. The remaining activity will involve serving the public during those hours the restaurant doors are open for business.

A regular schedule and routine should be established for both of these periods outside of the public hours. It is particularly desirable to have a definite routine for cleanup at the end of the serving day since, after a busy day of service, there is a great temptation to hold work over to the following day especially when one is closing up a restaurant late in the evening.

Generally, putting off cleanup until the next day will be a mistake. Among more obvious things to be done before the restaurant is closed down for the night are finishing washing and stacking of dishes, cleaning of pots and pans, kitchen

83

cleanup and a general cleanup of the dining room. This work will put the premises in the best possible condition for quick sprucing up and proper start-up of the operation on the following day.

### Pre-Opening Activities

Since the selling period for the restaurant is the hours when the restaurant is open to the public, some scheduling on a staggered shift basis can result in a more effective presentation. A maitre d' or hostess can be scheduled to come in thirty minutes before the restaurant opens its doors so that he or she has time to check over the appearance of the dining room table settings, napkins, and to do similar jobs that insure presenting the proper image to the public when the doors open.

The employee assigned pre-opening chores can continue through the lunch hour and dinner hour, if both are served, or from the dinner hour through closing if only dinner is served. In addition to having the responsibility for the image of the "front of the house," this individual can also check in waiters' cash against the waiters' checks or perform one or two control or accounting functions as part of a close-down procedure.

The chef or cook can come in early to be sure that the kitchen is organized and the food properly prepared; he will then be in a position to leave after the evening dinner has been served, with a second cook carrying on through the late hour service to closing. The second cook will then be responsible for cleaning up the kitchen so it is ready for action when the kitchen help comes in the next morning.

It is preferable to take liquor inventories every night when the bar closes, and this should be a part of the close-down procedure at the end of the operating day.

From these comments it should be obvious that a woman hired as a hostess or a man hired as a maitre d' should be

84

something more than one who just "looks good." This individual should be people-oriented, have an inquisitive, discerning eye, and a sense of proportion and propriety.

## The Weekly Meeting

The Navy has an excellent expression, "A happy ship," and your staff should be trained, oriented, and exposed to a leadership attitude designed to develop a strong esprit de corps among all of the employees. A restaurant is too small a business to allow for conflicts of personalities or for lack of a cohesive attitude; these will have the inevitable adverse impact upon atmosphere and performance in the operation.

An excellent device to help develop such a constructive mind is a weekly staff meeting attended by the manager and the personnel from the front of the house, such as the hostess, waitresses, waiters, bartenders, and probably also by the chef; and a second staff meeting with the kitchen personnel, probably attended by the hostess or maître d'.

These meetings should be organized in advance and should last only a half hour or so during which performance can be discussed and problems, which have been observed or may be anticipated, can be smoothed out. During these sessions each individual can have an opportunity to present suggestions as well as gripes.

As a matter of fact, one of the most important elements of such get-togethers is the proper airing of gripes or problems; the astute manager will also use this opportunity to compliment, in the presence of fellow workers, the effective employee or the employee who has made some particular contribution to the image of service. The smart manager, however, will scrupulously avoid giving the staff a feeling that any one employee is favored over another.

85

## Days Off to Recharge

Key personnel, particularly the manager, the chef, and the hostess or maitre d', should be scheduled with at least one full day off each week and at least two full weeks of vacation each year. Both they and their families need this change of pace to recharge their batteries and recreate their attitudes and spirits. The business of serving the public is a very exacting, difficult, and exasperating business at times; and only a fool will attempt to work day in and day out, or to require key people to work continuously, without realizing that this is neither efficient nor beneficial to the business in the long run.

The manager who moves about and sees what is being done by the competition gains other advantages as he can adapt good points and avoid the mistakes of others. A good relief manager, therefore, is a must. Often an effective arrangement can be worked out, through training and scheduling. For example, the hostess can function as a relief manager and the manager can function as a part-time maitre d'. An added advantage to this arrangement is that the manager gets to live with the problems in the front of the house while the employee being replaced is receiving time off.

## Customer Priorities

It has been well established that in order of importance those factors that contribute to the success of a restaurant operation are: (1) atmosphere; (2) service; and (3) appearance and quality of food. While this does not mean that bad food will be acceptable, it does imply a priority in the minds of most customers.

If you will recall the many restaurants you have visited, you will no doubt agree that you have gone back many times to the restaurant where the personnel was attentive, courteous, and service-oriented, although the food might not have been the most outstanding that you had ever encountered. On the other hand, you have gone to restaurants where the food was excellent but the service lacking and decided that you certainly did not want to go back to that particular establishment.

The atmosphere of concern or hospitality, indicative of a service-oriented attitude, begins the moment the customer walks through the door. The maitre d' or hostess should develop the faculty of recognizing repeat customers and welcoming them by name if they are regulars.

All of us like to feel important and when a gentleman brings his family members, friends, or business associates into a restaurant and is met with a salutation such as, "Good evening Mr. Jones, it's so good to see you again," or some similar friendly greeting, he feels important, impressed, and, as a result, is likely to return to this establishment.

## Service Starts with Seating

Also contributing to the hospitality image is care on the part of the hostess as to where people are placed when they are directed to a table.

There are a number of situations that are often repeated in restaurant seating that detract immeasurably from the image of thoughtful service. One of the most common occurs when a restaurant is crowded and requires couples to stack up in line while groups of four are seated in order to make maximum use of all chairs. This also happens with groups of five or more. They may also be required to wait while other parties arriving later are seated, eat, and even leave the restaurant. In this situation, the couple or larger group may be left waiting for a table merely because of the size of their party.

This treatment gives the impression that the restaurant is so profit-oriented and has a strong desire to get every last ounce of seating capacity used that the management is willing to put the customer's feelings and convenience to one side; it conveys a definite "customer be damned" image. As a matter of hospitable service, it is most important, that customers be seated as quickly as possible and in the order in which they come into the restaurant.

A customer may put up with delayed eating once or twice, but invariably it will drive him away; when service is attentive and prompt it will be appreciated and will result in a steady or repeat customer.

The way in which he is seated can be a factor in creating an impression that the customer is special. The effective maitre d' or hostess develops the faculty of quickly sizing up a party, then tries to use some consideration in selecting the table to which the party is directed.

On a light night when the restaurant will not sell all its tables, it is much more considerate to put a couple at a four-chair table rather than to insist upon their sitting at a "deuce." No couple minds sitting at a deuce when a restaurant is filled because all reasonable people recognize that the restaurant must get maximum use from its facilities.

On the other hand, on a slow night, while the couple perhaps will not complain at being placed at a deuce, they will certainly appreciate the thoughtfulness of providing them with a little more elbow room and a little more feeling of space and comfort by seating them at a "four" since this will obviously not deprive other customers of an opportunity to be promptly seated.

It is also better to seat a young couple on a date or a husband and wife, obviously on a "special night out," in an area where there is privacy, rather than to seat them in the most heavily traveled part of the dining room. Part of the charm of an evening out for these people is the ability to enjoy a feeling of privacy.

Also, seating a couple next to a group of four or six young men out for a night of fun and frolic does not exhibit good judgment. It is much better that these two types of parties be placed in sections of the dining room apart from one another.

A large family group—Mom, Dad, two or three children with Grandmother and Grandfather can best be placed in an alcove, a corner, or any similar location. This is especially true if children are quite small. At a table somewhat apart, their meal will not be ruined by their becoming the center of attention from surrounding tables if a child begins to act up a bit. Also when the family is placed in such a location only a minimum number of adjacent customers will be irritated by or exposed to such a distraction.

A little attentiveness on the part of a hostess or maitre d' in helping the party get settled, particularly when there are infants or aged people, will go a long way toward making them feel really at home and will increase the attractiveness and popularity of your establishment.

If the restaurant has a particularly good or interesting "special" and it is the practice for the hostess to distribute menus at the table as soon as the party is seated, she can —in a helpful and confiding tone—make a comment such as, "The dinner steak is particularly good today," or "We have special potato pancakes today that you might enjoy." When children are involved, she can also mention that children's portions are available at one-half the standard dinner rate or describe whatever situation is appropriate.

From the time the people in a party sit down and have a minute or two to look at the menu, they should receive attentive service. There should be no prolonged gaps in the service. If you operate the team system, a busboy, waiter, or waitress should immediately deliver bread, butter, water, and possibly a

89

salad if the menu is so constructed, to the table. At the same time, cocktail orders should be taken.

## When Customers Complain

If the party does not desire cocktails, the waitress should be trained to say, "Are you ready to order dinner?" and take the order promptly. It is very disconcerting to have a waitress come to a table to request a cocktail order and, when informed that the party is not desirous of ordering cocktails, have the waitress turn around and walk away without another word. The party is often kept waiting for several minutes, which seem like hours, before another waitress comes up to take the order. This sort of situation is completely unnecessary, and when the service staff operates as a team, it will never happen.

We continually talk about training, for although training may cost a few dollars, it definitely cannot be underrated at any level, from the porter on up through the manager. There will be times when, through no fault of the house, a customer will justifiably or unjustifiably feel as though he has not received the kind of service or quality of food that he expected. These complaints will more often than not be the result of an occasional poor cut of meat getting through or a "something wrong with the food" type of problem. The only approach to be used in such an instance is for the hostess, maitre d', or manager to come to the table, to inquire sympathetically as to the problem, and offer to remove the food in question and permit the customer to order something else.

If the complaint is made after the food has been consumed, or partially consumed, and the complainant does not wish to reorder, an apology should be extended whether the house is at fault or not. The item should be deleted from the check, with the comment that "We are apologetic and we hope that you will realize that this is not representative of our quality of service and will come back again . . ."

90

This treatment has on many occasions won a loyal customer while failure to extend this consideration has lost a customer forever. A young executive and his wife used to go for brunch every Sunday after church to a local hotel, part of a well-known chain. One Sunday morning the meat item ordered by the man was not properly done and he requested that the waitress return it to the kitchen to be cooked properly. Leaving all of the vegetables and other items on the table, the waitress returned the meat to the kitchen where it was cut up into little pieces, fried in a frying pan, and returned to the plate, which the waitress brought back to the table.

What had happened was very obvious, and even if the meat had been properly prepared, by then the vegetables and other items were cold. The young man, without eating further, immediately and quietly asked for the check. This should have been a tip-off to even the most obtuse service personnel that the situation was going badly. He went to the cashier's counter to pay his check before leaving.

On the way he happened to pass by the manager and, in a very polite way, said to the manager, "I think you should be aware that this situation has occurred," and described in detail what had happened. The manager's response was, "Thank you for telling me." The man paid his check and left.

No offer was made on the part of the manager to delete this customer's part of the check. Actually, under those circumstances, since the meal was ruined for the entire party, our recommendation would have been for the manager to pick up the entire check, apologize, and invite the party to come back another time.

Because of this episode, the young executive vowed never to return to that particular restaurant, and has been heard to say many times since that he has not returned to that particular dining room; in addition, he has refused to go into any dining room in any location owned by the hotel chain.

91

Since this man is a young executive who travels extensively, the financial loss resulting from this one customer due to the ineptitude of the service personnel in that restaurant will add up to many hundreds of dollars.

Another loss accrues from the adverse impact upon the reputation and image of the hotel chain generated as the story is passed on by the individual to his friends and acquaintances.

A dramatic illustration of the other side of the coin occurred in a restaurant providing a luncheon for a group of twenty secretaries. Upon completion of the meal, four of the women complained that there was something wrong with their food. Upon checking, the manager determined that the food had been improperly prepared due to some oversight on the part of a new kitchen employee. He proceeded to apologize, explaining that this was not typical of his service, and asking that all consider themselves his guests for that meal.

The impact of this manager's gesture was so dramatic that his restaurant became the site of all future luncheons for the local secretarial association, and the goodwill created was carried in stories far and wide, resulting in some of the best advertising this restaurant had ever experienced.

### Bringing Customers Back

It should not be necessary to talk about the importance of hot food being hot and cold food being cold, and food being delivered to the table as described on the menu. Too often eggs and toast are delivered cold; coffee pots are left standing until the coffee is lukewarm or cold; and food described on the menu as "hot apple pie with melted cheese" comes out as ice cold apple pie with a slice of cheese dropped on top.

When your customer comes to the restaurant, you should be concerned with more than just a one-time sale. Your whole presentation should be aimed at convincing him that this is the sort of place he's always been looking for, with the result that he should come back again, and again, and again.

One of the principles of selling in the automobile business, as well as in many other businesses, is to sell the customer "up." You sell your restaurant customer "up" by providing him with the type of service and food that will convince him that he should eat in your restaurant not just once, but many times, and should bring his friends and family back on subsequent visits.

It is difficult to understand, but I'm sure every reader has had the unpleasant experience of being treated by restaurant personnel as though he were a bother, an interruption, or an inconvenience simply because he came into the restaurant. The attitude adopted by personnel will be determined by the enthusiasm and actions of the manager.

### Managers Set Style

If the manager demonstrates by his actions and interest how keenly he feels about good service, this will be reflected all the way down the line. Customers sense these things too and a smiling attitude and gracious, hospitable service will bring profits from repeat and recommended business.

One of the fundamental mistakes made by too many restaurant operators is not making the small effort needed to reap a harvest of extra profits. Each minute that your restaurant is open it should be recognized that, every hour of every day of every week, it is engaged in a sales program that includes selling. Every time a hostess or waitress or a busboy walks up to a table, he is making a sales call. Sincerity in the sales appeal is most effective and costs nothing.

Upon completion of the main course, does the waitress tally up the check and place it face down on the table without inquiring as to whether anyone would care for a dessert or an after-dinner drink? Much, much too often!

Does the waiter carry a book of matches or lighter so that if a customer asks for a match or light, his request can be promptly attended to? Too often such a request results in a response such as, "Gee, I don't have any, I'll see if I can locate some for you," with a possibility that the waiter might be back in five or ten minutes with a partially filled book of matches.

How much more satisfying and ego-building when a gentleman places a cigar in his mouth, if a waiter or maitre d' immediately responds with a cigarette lighter and offers a light.

A friend who eats out frequently, and who happens to enjoy drinking iced tea the year-round, regularly goes through the following exercise in most restaurants during the months between September and May. He will politely ask the waiter or waitress when his beverage choice is requested if he might have some iced tea, provided it isn't a lot of extra work. (The last phrase obviously is meant as a gesture of politeness and consideration.) Almost always the response is: "We do not serve iced tea except in the summer months." He then responds with the request that he receive a pot of hot tea and a glass of ice and, invariably, he is provided with a pot of hot water, a teabag, and a glass of ice, with the result that he has his iced tea.

Employees dedicated to service would recognize that no great effort is involved when the waitress or waiter makes up hot tea, or drops a teabag in a pot of hot water, letting it steep while going about serving the other beverages, and then pours it into a glass filled with ice cubes and delivers that to the table. The result is recognition on the part of the customer that a little extra effort has been made on his behalf, and the impression is most favorable. It will, more often than not, result in a larger tip.

There are so many examples of indifferent service, and they are so widely experienced that they have come to represent the mainstream of the restaurant business to many people. These are the experiences that have prompted the many, many stories and complaints that service just isn't what it used to be.

Don't let your restaurant be the restaurant dramatized in the story about the waiter who was involved in an automobile accident and was rushed to the emergency room at the local hospital. As he was being wheeled in on the table, a doctor was passing nearby and the waiter feebly raised his hand to get the doctor's attention. The doctor continued to hurry on his way, calling back, "Sorry, not my table."

# Hiring
# Personnel

# 10

There are several steps involved in finding the right man or woman for the right job. Although these seem to apply universally, they seem to be more neglected in the restaurant business than they do in manufacturing and other endeavors.

Once the flow of materials through your restaurant has been established as part of your overall planning and you have determined the number of employees you will hire and the jobs they will fill, it is then appropriate to analyze each job and provide a description of what is going to be expected of the employee while doing that job.

Having determined the content of the job, which will, in turn, assist in determining the pay scale to be set for the job, you are then faced with the problem of recruiting, selecting,

97

and hiring. This process, hopefully, will be followed by a training program, a subject discussed in the next chapter.

When you face the problem of hiring, you are concerned first with obtaining qualified people; and, second, with a continuous supply of people as they are needed in the future.

You want the right person for the right job because you hope to develop an efficient, happy organization. In the restaurant business it does not necessarily follow, except for one or two key jobs such as chef and cook, that an employee with a restaurant background is a necessary or even the most desirable type of employee. There are many kinds of employees who can fill your job requirements.

## Where to Find Help

If you are an individual entrepreneur or one of a small investment group going ahead with a single restaurant, your problems will be different from those of a large corporation involved in diversifying into the restaurant or food business or expanding its food line in this direction.

The one thing you should avoid like the plague in either instance is nepotism, the hiring of relatives (except in the close-knit family operation of an individual restaurant) or friends, since employees from either category are not apt to contribute in a way that produces the best results.

For the corporation, usually the most immediate source of good employees is from your present satisfied employees. Some of these may wish to take advantage of the opportunity to move in a new direction or new field, particularly if the job is presented as a part of an atmosphere of opportunity or advancement.

It is also true that your employees may have friends who are looking for employment and whom they would recommend highly. There is no problem in encouraging employees to recommend friends and acquaintances; this is often a legitimate source of excellent recruits.

Obviously, educational institutions such as local high schools, colleges, or trade schools are other potential sources. It should be recognized, however, that a letter to such an institution is almost a waste of time. If you are going to use an educational institution as a source for employees, the proper approach is to visit the institution and talk to the dean of students and other officials. Become acquainted with these people, and make them acquainted with your objectives and needs; in other words, develop a relationship.

You will find that the time and effort spent in this manner will generate referrals and positive results, while anything less than this approach to the educational institution is ineffective.

We have found that usually an excellent source of employees is a nearby military base or military installation, although such sources are not always available.

Spouses of service personnel and service personnel who wish to moonlight by taking second jobs, providing that they are permitted by local regulations to do so, are an excellent source of employees. They are excellent because they usually are good workers with a good sense of discipline. Furthermore, as the relationship is established, the word tends to be passed on automatically as some people leave and others arrive at the base, assuring a continuous flow of very good people.

In many instances, these people have had experience working in officers' clubs, mess halls, and other facilities. We cannot overemphasize the value of a visit to the local military base in an effort to become acquainted with the enlisted division officer, the station administrative personnel officer, or other appropriate officer who is in a position to assist you and assist those within the organization who are looking for extra work. You will find these people to be extremely cooperative.

### Employment Agencies

Employment agencies generally fall into two categories: public employment agencies that are free of charge and private employment agencies that collect a fee for finding jobs.

Public employment agencies generally are expanding their services and normally are a source of good employees for the unskilled jobs associated with your business. Private employment agencies require enough development of a relationship to enable you to establish an appraisal of their credibility.

Some private agencies are essentially irresponsible in their approach to the business of placing employees while others are excellent and do a good deal of screening. Their efforts give you a higher level of assurance that you're getting the kind of employee that you really want.

It is worthwhile, particularly for skilled and middle management jobs, to have established a relationship with a good private employment agency.

When you request a private agency to locate an individual for you, you should make sure to extend the courtesy, both to the individual and to the agency, of interviewing each individual who is presented. After the individual is presented, it is desirable to have a conference either by telephone or in person with the agency representative to tell him where he missed the mark if the individual is not acceptable.

You will find that after having gone through two or three of these exercises the placement specialist will begin to identify very closely with what type of individual you are looking for. He will then be in a position to provide you with a very, very valuable service that will save you a lot of time and effort and will give you a measure of assurance that the people you are hiring are of the caliber you desire and have the skill you are seeking.

100

.   One of the many typical companies specializing in this area is Roth-Young, Inc., a company that provides placement services to the foodservice industry through offices in some fifteen or more cities throughout the country.

*Interesting Your Local Community.*   A proper amount of social and civic activity on your part, or on the part of management personnel, will generate interest in your company and increase the number who come to your door seeking employment opportunities.

Activities that develop such contacts might be newcomers clubs, university clubs, veterans organizations, as well as the local chamber of commerce and service clubs. The individual in this business who does not belong to the local chamber of commerce and the local convention bureau or board of trade is very shortsighted indeed.

### College Students Part-Time

You may desire, once you're established, to create a backlog of people who are interested in part-time or temporary work. Such a list enables you to fill a temporary emergency need very quickly and to pick up the additional help that you need for peak periods, holidays, and other exceptionally busy times.

It has been our experience that college students on their vacations or during recess periods, represent an excellent source of intelligent workers who perform at a high standard. Relationships can often be established with a number of students for the duration of their college attendance, insuring that they are available to you during each holiday season, for example, for three or four years in a row.

Another advantage of hiring students is that normally they pass the word on to associates and friends, and when they themselves are no longer available you usually find, that

101

through their references, others are standing in line waiting to take their positions.

A ready supply of available students also gives you an opportunity to cover an emergency requirement created by the departure of a full-time employee until that employee can be effectively replaced.

Contrary to the view of most people, it has been pretty well established that classified ads in newspapers are not the best recruiting tool. Normally, they are used only as a last resort.

## The Selection Process

After having provided for a flow of potential employees, your next step will be the selection process. The object of this process, obviously, is to choose from a group of applicants the one person best qualified to fill the job. The more complicated and demanding the job, the greater the number of applicants you will generally need to interview. It is desirable to interview at least three to five applicants for most jobs. However, if a good, well-qualified applicant shows up at the outset, there is no reason to risk losing this applicant to another employer or delay the filling of the job in order to arbitrarily go through the motions of interviewing three or four more people.

The selection process is like running the applicants through a series of meshes; the first one is large, letting through most of the applicants, then the next one becomes finer, so that in selecting the final, successful candidate, you eventually reach the level of refinement dictated by the quality of the applicants.

The process will involve the pre-selection interview. This is a brief interview essentially designed to remove from consideration the obviously unsuited applicants. These interviews do not have to be conducted by the individual responsible for the hiring and should take only a few minutes. Most of those talked to at this stage will not even be asked to complete an application form. It's important to remember that the first step in the interview process is not, as is often the case, the completion of a job application form; but rather it is a brief meeting in order to show the courtesy of attention to the individual coming in and to give the interviewing person an opportunity to size up the applicant quickly. The interviewer can then determine whether filling out an application is in the interest of either the management or the applicant.

### When the Applicant Looks Good

The interviewer can take the name and address of the applicant, but if the applicant does not have the qualifications for the job involved, the interviewer may simply thank the applicant for the visit and for the management's future reference make a brief notation as to the reason for this person's unsuitability.

If the applicant is suited, however, you, as the manager, then should go on to explain what the job requirements will be; and, of course, to do this effectively you have to know the hours to be worked, salary, duties, and other facts about the job.

You should then go on to explain the job benefits. These should not be limited only to the salary, hours, number of days the employee works, whether or not there is accident and health insurance or vacation involved; you should also indicate your concern for your people by describing such things as lunchroom facilities, opportunity for promotion, whether or not the work is likely to be steady or seasonal, and any hidden factors which the average applicant could not anticipate until he became familiar with the operation.

For example, if there are physical discomforts associated with a particular job — until the individual has become accustomed to the time and motion required, it is appropriate to say that the employees ". . . normally find it a little bit uncomfortable for three or four days while getting used to the job, but this will pass away and not be a problem to you."

If there is a requirement to wear a uniform or a hairnet the individual should be informed. Any other restrictions of this sort should also be discussed.

If you are seeking applicants for a steady position and you are expecting them to go on with you on a permanent basis, hopefully to advance, one condition that calls for extra consideration in screening the applicant should be: repeated job changes and job hopping without adequate explanation. This could indicate that the individual is either unstable or has a problem in achieving social acceptability from his fellow employees.

In the past, interviewers have regarded a prior income higher than that offered by the new job as reason to "knock out" an applicant. We do not necessarily agree with this reasoning because of the nature of the economy in recent years. We recommend that in the event an individual is taking a cut in salary, this matter be discussed frankly with him, primarily to determine whether or not he is going to be able to maintain an appropriate standard of living in the job you are offering.

Rather than the cut in salary necessarily making the applicant unhappy and prompting him to look for another job while he's working for you, it may and, in many cases, does prompt him to work for you in such a manner as to deserve rapid promotion in order to bring his salary back to its prior level. Therefore, it is our feeling that a previously higher income can be an asset and is not necessarily always a detraction, contrary to the opinion held by some.

Divorce or separation at the time of applying for a job can indicate a period of emotional instability, although the social changes that have taken place in our society in recent years

104

have tended to modify the seriousness of this problem in many cases. It is our feeling that this type of situation is merely an indicator of need for further in-depth investigation as opposed to an automatic disqualification.

### If He's Failed in His Own Business

Many individuals who are in the hiring business say that people who have failed in businesses of their own should be automatically knocked out of the running. On the contrary, some of the best employees we have had the pleasure of working with are employees who have attempted to go into business for themselves — an indication of a high degree of initiative — but for a variety of reasons were unable to make it. Frequently the reason is that they did not start with sufficient capital to succeed in their own business. We are aware of a senior vice-president of one of the largest corporations in the world who went bankrupt several years ago running his own restaurant. He determined to work off the bankruptcy indebtedness and went to work for a corporation at a middle-management level, eventually working himself up to the top management, senior vice-president level, and being a very valuable contributor.

We are sure that the experience of failing in business on the part of an individual, particularly in these economic times, can be a tremendous asset. An individual with such experience truly becomes a part of a team, although working for someone else. Oftentimes this experience gives him an appreciation for the advantages of such an affiliation which is far beyond that of the employee who has not failed in his own business.

Obviously, workers who are in off-season situations, such as construction workers, or workers who are available because they are on strike elsewhere present considerable reason for reflection on the part of the hiring authority because of the temporary nature of their availability and also because their primary concern will be with matters other than the job for which they are applying.

### Screen-Outs

In your interview you will want to determine the individual applicant's energy level. This can be done by noting whether he appears to be an energetic person; whether he engages in activities such as sports or hobbies that require a high interest and energy level; whether he seeks to improve his lot in life by seeking a better job than his previous or present one; and whether he shows the level of interest and energy to do a good job of filling the application out completely as opposed to slowing down and becoming sloppy halfway through.

An aggressive individual will generally respond to questions in ways that indicate he is pleased in situations which give him the opportunity to lead, direct, or supervise others; over-aggressiveness might be indicated by sharply expressed response to criticism. Any arbitrary disregard for instructions on the application form should be a definite negative factor.

We do not necessarily share the high degree of confidence some employers have placed in aptitude tests. We feel that verified performance records have a great deal of validity in determining people's adaptability and potential. Also, we feel that aptitude tests represent only one factor for consideration and are as often misused and misinterpreted as they are effectively used and interpreted.

We have also had the experience of finding the nature of certain jobs was such that low scores on certain types of aptitude tests were more desirable than high scores. Consequently, many employees who received unfavorable recommendations from the personnel testing them turned out to be the best accomplishers in certain jobs, whereas those who received the highest recommendations turned out to be wholly unsuited to these same jobs.

In any event, aptitude tests, other than skill tests such as typing tests and dexterity tests for certain types of jobs, should be approached with a great deal of caution in terms of the

106

amount of impact they should properly have upon your hiring decisions.

### Evaluation Interview

After you have screened out applicants in a series of initial interviews, you will then go on with the remaining applicants in the evaluation interview which requires a good deal more consideration and skill than the initial interview does.

Two major pitfalls in the evaluation interview often encountered by interviewers are: (1) letting some personal characteristic that would have no effect whatever on the employee's ability to do a job cause them to give a negative recommendation; or (2) permitting some outstanding characteristic, such as a likeable personality, that appears attractive to the interviewer but has no reference to the abilities needed to perform the job, influence a favorable vote.

In order to build up the confidence of prospective employees so that they will open up and reveal their true feelings regarding the employment opportunity under discussion, the interviewer is going to have to combine good sales techniques with a basic sensitivity to human feelings. The latter will enable the interviewer to grasp the implications of changes in voice inflection, facial expression, focus on the eyes. A person who interviews job candidates must also have adaptability. This quality is important since it enables one to change pace and adapt to the differences in individual applicants' temperaments, degrees of poise, and other characteristics. Maturity is still another quality necessary to make an objective evaluation and analysis and to avoid pitfalls such as those mentioned above.

Employment interviews fall into three basic types: (1) the patterned or formulated interview; (2) the uncontrolled interview, in which the dialogue with the applicant may range far

107

and wide, on the basis that uncontrolled dialogue will uncover significant facts; and (3) the controlled interview, really a compromise between the other two.

### Controlled Interview

In the controlled interview, which we favor, the formulated list of questions is eliminated but the interviewer substitutes a general discussion exploring the areas that these questions would have covered. This type of interview should be conducted in a manner that assists the interviewer in coming to a conclusion as to the applicant's attitude, motivation, and adaptability.

The concern is with exploring such things as the applicant's work experience, educational background, outside interests and hobbies, and the quality of his home life.

Finally, you should check the references of applicants. This checking can be done most easily by calling the former supervisor of the job applicant. In making such a check, however, it is wise to be cautious if the applicant indicates that a change is being made under circumstances which are other than favorable. Be realistic in determining how much the attitude of the supervisor, as you detect from this person's approach on the telephone, was a contributing factor to this change. Evaluating this factor will help establish the level of credibility to be given to the comments made by the job applicant's prior supervisor.

If you find that an individual supervisor is very caustic and negative with regard to the applicant, it is probably wise to call and check a number of other references to see whether the playback is warranted. In this way you can be sure the individual is not being deprived of an opportunity to perform for you and that you are not being deprived of a desirable employee because of some personality-oriented situation.

108

Employment application forms should be kept as simple and succinct as possible. They should contain only the data needed as a basis for the employee's permanent personnel record.

After successfully completing these interviews, the employee is hired and welcomed aboard; the training experience is then set in motion.

# Receiving
# and Training
# Personnel

# 11

You should always remember that business and people go together; they're inseparable and it's impossible for either to survive economically without the other. The principal factor involved in all products and services sold today is labor; the cost and the quality of each product is related directly to the use and contribution of labor.

Good operators are constantly aware of this fact and seek to get the most for the money they pay by carefully selecting all personnel and adequately training them on a continuing basis for the work to be done. In this manner these operators protect their investment by providing the kind of supervisory assistance that will help workers do a better and more efficient job and, at the same time, maintain their confidence and interest in their jobs.

The best employees have confidence in the company they work for and have respect for its management. They acquire loyalty to their employer and interest in their jobs as a matter of response to leadership. This attitude is a fitting tribute to the effectiveness of supervisory personnel and management but it does not come about accidentally. Respect and loyalty must be earned by those who are in charge and who, consequently, represent the company and its policies.

The process begins with the payment of proper wages and benefits for the job to be done and extends to the provision of effective training and supervision, thus ensuring that the job is well done and that the cost of getting it done stays in line with all other costs.

Getting along with people is often called "labor relations" and, while specific obligations of employees and employers are often spelled out in labor contracts or various labor laws, successful operations can, and most often do, depend upon the relationship developed between the supervisory personnel and the worker. Mutual respect and mutual understanding are vital.

Your products and your efforts are going to be specialized and under the constant scrutiny of your customers. Your job in this business is to satisfy many types of people by catering to an infinite variety of tastes and preferences. At the same time your product has to have some reasonable uniformity in order to facilitate its effective and economical production.

Therefore, you need the full and willing service and participation of the people you employ. Each employee must be trained in your methods and procedures and the employee must be periodically retrained in order to maintain interest and motivation and to achieve quality performance.

Personnel training, to be sure, is time-consuming and costly; therefore, it is important that the effort invested in training an employee not be wasted. It is also important that you recognize that it is much more costly to replace an employee through recruiting and training a new one than it is to retrain and motivate an existing employee.

You should establish some uniform set of regulations regarding the policy which you intend to follow among all employees with regard to: working hours; recording the hours worked; overtime policy; grooming and uniform regulations; meals and eating on the job; pay raises and salary advances; sick leave; medical examinations; parking regulations; and other similar controlling rules.

No rule or regulation should be promulgated unless it is to be uniformly enforced. Remember that a rule or regulation that is not uniformly enforced is worse than no regulation at all.

## Job Description

You should also provide a simple job description for each key job so the individual knows what is expected of him and by what measure his performance will be gauged.

For example, a typical job description for a steward might read as follows:

> *The steward is charged with the responsibility of ordering all products and supplies required for the conduct of operations. He must see that ordering is done in accordance with the prescribed accounting procedures and purchasing procedures, using company purchase order forms provided for this purpose —and see that the purchase order forms are properly completed for each transaction. He is responsible for items received being checked in, with a check of grade, quantity, and type —and that a record is made as to the place of warehousing or storage with the operation or the routing from receiving.*

113

*He should maintain an accurate file of all purchasing activity, forwarding completed and extended purchase orders for processing.*

*He should cooperate in the completion of inventories and all purchases should be made in accordance with the established purchasing routine, from approved vendors provided for by management.*

*He is also responsible to report failures by suppliers to live up to their agreements, and he reports directly to the restaurant manager and is considered a member of the manager's staff.*

You can readily see that a two or three paragraph description of this sort prepared in advance, perhaps during the construction phase as you plan your total operation and its staffing, and then put into a loose-leaf binder for use by the manager, will be an excellent tool. It will insure that the operation will in fact unfold as has been intended and that uniformity of employment effort will be attained without the jobs varying according to each incumbent manager as the manager changes.

Another typical job description could be that of a chef/kitchen supervisor; and it could read somewhat as follows:

*Kitchen supervisor reports to the restaurant manager and is considered a member of his staff.*

*He is responsible for maintaining close supervision over all of the work in the production area of the restaurant or the 'back of the house.'*

*He is intended to be (or not to be) a member of the working crew and is responsible for keeping his manager informed relative to all matters concerning the efficient and productive operation of the kitchen.*

114

*He does not make policy decisions but will advise the manager on matters such as menu, arrangement, daily requirements of perishable supplies, meat, and other product requirements.*

*He supervises and schedules the efforts of the kitchen crew and personnel.*

*He is responsible for portion control and waste control and for the maintenance of proper food handling procedures.*

*He is responsible for maintaining accuracy in preparing orders and is responsible for appearance, attractiveness, freshness of preparation.*

*He supervises the housekeeping and provides for the care and maintenance of the equipment.*

*He supervises the drawing of storeroom supplies; maintains a recipe file; supervises the preparation of cooked ingredients and assembly of orders.*

Again, you see that the areas of responsibility for the chef/kitchen supervisor have been clearly defined so that this person, as well as everybody else, knows what these areas of responsibility should be.

## Controls

The key to profits, all other things being in order, is the imposition of a sound system of controls. Many a restaurant operation has been destroyed by a failure to impose a proper system of controls early in the game and to insist upon compliance with the system by all employees. Appropriate detail may vary from restaurant to restaurant, depending upon size, complexity of menu, and other variables, but the fundamental principles of an effective controls system are universally applicable.

115

To provide a jumping off point for the restaurant operator designing his own system, we will demonstrate here the fundamentals of a sound system.

Everything begins with the menu. As the menu is established (see discussion of menu planning on page 29 and following) the various foods, spices, and other items necessary to create the selections listed on the menu are simultaneously established.

As soon as the menu is firmed, the items listed should be prepared, and portioned. As this is done each of the entrees is priced, including allowance for waste, shrinkage, and other such considerations. Given this food cost verification, the pricing on the menu can be verified to support the projected food cost target, for example 38 percent, 42 percent, or whatever figure has been determined.

This level of planning establishes the amount of food in raw form required to produce each menu item; and, if this area of the business is controlled, then your planning will lead to a food cost as estimated or projected. This is, however, a big IF.

You will achieve your projected food cost if the four following conditions are met.

1. If foods ordered are of the same grades and in the same amounts as those actually delivered and received;

2. If the food delivered and stored is monitored throughout its storage to prevent spoilage and throwaway;

3. If the food is handled in such a manner as to avoid a widespread practice of its being taken home by kitchen help;

4. If quantities designed into the menu are adhered to and food is not wasted in the preparation process.

116

When you consider these "ifs," you can readily appreciate the many pitfalls involved in ensuring that the predicted food cost becomes the actual food cost.

Once the menu design and portion control base are established, a system for ordering should be placed in force. Preferably, this system should be based upon a three-part ordering form which the person maintaining control can use for ordering food items in order to replenish inventory reductions incurred through production in the kitchen. In other words, have the kitchen help work from a par inventory that lists requirements for kitchen production.

So that a proper check of the items ordered can be made, ascertaining that they have in fact been delivered and received in the ordered grade, number, and specification, a second copy of the form should go to receiving.

Now we have established three fundamentals of a good system of controls: (1) proper portion and menu planning; (2) independent ordering authority; (3) proper receiving and documentation of items ordered.

The next integral step is to provide for proper in-house storage and inventory control. Obviously, given the perishable nature of foodstuffs, the system must be a "first in, first out" inventory system.

The inventory control responsibility can be assigned to the chef or, preferably, to a steward. Which method is used depends upon the nature of the particular restaurant involved.

Once the inventory-control elements are in place, the next step is to establish a method to monitor usage, that is, a summary, maintained at the dining room level, of tickets and items served and finally a cross-balance with cash at the end of each day.

What you have set up, then, is a system whereby you have a manufacturing operation in the kitchen, which buys

117

raw materials and produces a finished product, namely a menu entree. These are "sold" to the dining room, as though it were a retail outlet, and counted out of the kitchen through policing of the order tickets. The total number of items delivered to the dining room from the kitchen will lead to a quick calculation of food cost. A cross-check of this figure with inventory disappearance will verify the amount. If there is an excessive disappearance of inventory, then there is need for investigation of that problem.

At the other end of the system, a cross-check of the tickets with the cash in the register will provide a verification of delivery. Employee meals should be recorded on tickets. If the amount of food sent from the kitchen to the dining room and the amount of cash received from customers do not equate properly, then, again, there is a need to investigate.

The final element, which is significant, is that of monitoring the call for the items listed on the menu. A checkoff, either through the use of automatic recording cash registers or simply a checkoff to be done manually by the cashier will produce the information necessary to determine when items should be dropped from the menu, replaced, or revised. This system will enable you to keep a handle of customer acceptance as well as on quality control. Unexplained drop-offs of previously popular items demand immediate investigation.

By now you can see that a good control system has three basic loops. (For illustration, see appendix.)

1. The production cycle, which includes portioning, ordering, receiving, and cooking;

2. The delivery to dining room, sale by the restaurant, payment by customers, and accounting for cash;

3. The monitoring of customer appeal and quality control, as a basis for relating judgmental decisions to each of the other systems and as a means of provid-

118

ing "red flags" to alert the owner to bad trends or practices as soon as they begin.

To operate a restaurant without controls is like trying to operate an airplane without a fuel quantity gauge and a compass. Your accountant, or any auditor worth his salt, will tell you that controls which do not build in a check and balance system are not controls at all. You cannot afford to put your operation completely into the hands of a chef or chef manager; nor can you put it into the hands of a maitre d' or maitre d'/manager.

Think of your restaurant as two operations under a single roof. The kitchen, or so-called "back of the house," is the manufacturing operation; the dining room and bar area, or so-called "front of the house," is a retail outlet. Keeping these two operations balanced through the application of a sound system of internal product and cash control will be the most important thing that you can do to ensure profits continue long after you open your well-planned restaurant.

Even if you have the most well-planned operation and best menu ever to come into existence, and customers stand in line to get into your place, you will most likely go out of business if you do not have a system of internal controls. You will learn the harsh truth three to six months after you have actually gone bankrupt. Do not cut corners on this aspect!

## Staff Meetings

No individual manager is capable of properly doing everything necessary for a successful operation. It is, therefore, desirable that he extend his "eyes and ears" and "hands and feet" to cover all of the matters that require his attention.

A proven method of getting this overview is through regular staff meetings. For such meetings to be effective, the members of the staff should be informed, as previously indicated, as to what their jobs are and how these jobs relate to those of fellow staff members. A recurring appraisal of the operation is necessary; to effectively make an appraisal of the staff, the manager must conduct regular staff meetings.

In such meetings the progress of the operation is first reviewed, then corrective or improvement programs are scheduled and coordinated.

Staff meetings will also assist the manager in the important process of evaluating key personnel. The common denominator of success, as we have said, is people. Every one of your competitors can buy the same product and the same equipment that you can buy. The thing that makes you different or better is your people and the way you handle them.

Long-term growth requires that those employees who are with you now, and have potential for the future, be developed. To accomplish this, you have to know what their strong and weak points are so that you can provide opportunities that strengthen their weak areas and that take advantage of their strong areas.

You must also insure that no level of personnel is subject to the whimsical pressure of personal conflict. To prevent this problem, the manager should regularly evaluate his key personnel on some type of simple key personnel evaluation form which enables him to correlate all evaluations made by supervisory personnel.

This function is very important and regular adherence to its accomplishment should be insisted upon. Such evaluations should be done abut twice a year and certainly not less often than once a year.

# Getting the Most Out of Your People

# 12

The first day on the job is unquestionably the most important to every new employee regardless of the level at which he is hired. It is essential that the supervisor recognize this fact as such knowledge will enable him to effectively organize the "break in" period to make the most of this time, when all of the factors are at their very best, to win loyalty, stimulate interest, and rapidly get the employee into full production.

In order to accomplish these aims effectively, you first have to get yourself ready to receive the new employee. To do this you should quickly review his education, experience, and training and have the contents of his job in mind. You should also have a description of his job ready for him to review upon his arrival. His work place and his equipment should be ready too.

Upon his arrival you should welcome the new employee, put him at ease, and show a genuine interest in him. Introduce yourself and identify his relationship to you and to any other individuals with whom he will have a direct working relationship, particularly a supervisory relationship.

Explain the overall function of the operation to him. How does he fit into the total organization; and what part will he play on this team. To whom will he report? Introduce him to his supervisor. Show him around the place; explain the layout of the building. Don't forget to explain the location of restrooms, the policy with regard to coffee breaks, and the facilities available to him for his rest periods. In other words, indicate a legitimate interest and concern for him and for getting him started on the right foot.

You should briefly cover the rules and regulations with which he will be concerned, such as hours of work, lunch periods, and breaks.

## Show and Tell

Next, you should take the time (and we cannot overemphasize the value of taking a sufficient amount of time for this) to prepare him and show him on a step-by-step basis the how, what, and why of his job. Test his ability, observe him, correct his errors and follow up.

Having done this, assign him a "big brother." There should be someone to whom he can turn for advice and assistance when he needs it. Then, as time goes on, and he is handling the job himself, check back periodically on his progress. Make corrections and give him guidance and encouragement. A failure to do these things will result in the employee's seeking a level that is acceptable, but that will invariably be a level less desirable than the one you would like to see him achieve. This less professional level of work will make it more difficult to raise him to higher levels in the future.

Just remember, your workers are people, and they have the same feelings and emotions which move you. When you think back to your first day on the job, you will recall that this was a time when you were most eager, most curious to learn, most anxious to please, most open-minded, and most ready to listen. This is the time when the "iron is hot." This is the time when the manager can invest an extra twenty minutes that will pay dividends from that day forward.

Good management and good customer relations are dependent on the sincere concern of the people who get the job done. Many individuals feel ill at ease in approaching the job of training a new worker. Some feel that the job this employee is to perform is so simple that it doesn't really require instruction. They fail to recognize that the individual employee may be approaching this job for the first time, and to that person it is not quite so simple.

## Timetable for Training

During World War II this country was faced with the herculean task of introducing into industry thousands of new employees who were unskilled and untrained. It was necessary to quickly fill the void left by thousands who were called into military service during this massive emergency.

Methods had to be devised to utilize people quickly and effectively. Certain universal principles were developed; these principles apply to every single situation involving the training of new workers.

The first universal principle is that before training is attempted you should get yourself ready to conduct the training. This preparation should include having a timetable, in other words, knowing how much knowledge or skill you want the trainees to have by what time. Obviously, a dishwasher, to be acceptable, must reach the required level of skill within a short span of time. This is quite different from what you will

123

require from a hostess of maitre d'. People in such more complex jobs will need more time if they are to accomplish their missions effectively as members of the team in your operation.

Secondly, you have to break the job down into units, listing the key points or steps in doing the job in their proper order or sequence. When you present the job on a step-by-step basis, indicate the reason why it is done this way. Emphasize, where appropriate, the impact on customer relations or safety, always good motivational key points.

When the worker arrives, have everything ready so that he has the correct tools and they are in good condition. He should have everything that he will need to get the job done correctly and effectively. Be sure the work place is properly arranged in the manner in which the worker is expected to keep it. Housekeeping is an important point to stress here.

The actual training of the worker should follow these specific, established steps.

1. Begin with the preparation of the worker, at which time you're putting him at ease, describing the work, and finding out how much he already knows about the job. Get him interested in learning the job correctly. Put him in the right position and in the right frame of mind.

2. Present the operation. Tell him; show him; illustrate each step in order, one step at a time. Stress each key point. Give only as much as he can master in one session; instruct and explain clearly, completely, and, above all, patiently.

3. Try his performance; have him do the job while you correct his errors as they occur, explaining what they are and why. If necessary, have him explain each point to you as he does the job and make sure that he understands what he is to do.

4. Finally, follow up by putting him on his own and giving him, as we suggested earlier, a "big brother," a person to whom he can turn for help.

5. Check frequently; encourage questions; taper off your coaching, then follow up.

## Retraining Conferences

After the employees in your restaurant have been trained you must provide a continuing retraining and motivational effort which should be built around conferences planned for two levels.

1. The manager's staff conferences with his key people, such as his hostess, maitre d', kitchen manager or executive chef, storeroom man or steward, if there is one.

2. Conferences between conferees from the manager's staff and their departments or the people they supervise. For example, the hostess or maitre d' should sit down with the waiters or waitresses once or twice a week, at the beginning or end of a working day, and informally review and discuss problems being faced in that part of the business, criticizing where necessary in a constructive way and complimenting where compliments are in order.

If you are going to conduct conferences, we urge you to conduct them properly and effectively. There is no better tool for you to use in the successful development of business than the conference; and yet there is no tool that is so universally misused and abused at all levels of management as the conference.

125

What is a good conference? It is a gathering of people who meet, formally or informally, to think out the best solutions to their common problems by pooling, in an informal discussion, their varying viewpoints, knowledge and experience.

## The Discussion Leader

The discussion should involve everybody but discussion does not occur just by getting people together. It requires an effective discussion leader and good discussion behavior.

The discussion leader ordinarily should have an agenda, preferably written, although in the informal conference with waitresses, waiters, or kitchen help, it may be unwritten; however, the points to be covered should be clear in his own mind.

The discussion leader will guide the discussion. He will start the ball rolling by making everybody aware of what problems are under discussion, and will see that no one participant dominates the discussion. He will keep facts and opinions separated; and, from time to time, will sum up main points made and brought out so that everyone will know where they have been, where they are, and where they are going.

He will plan the time and make it pay off by keeping the discussion on the topics under consideration.

He will attempt to develop among his people good discussion behavior, which includes a friendly and natural attitude characterized by objectivity and open-mindedness. He will see that each listens to the other person—and in this regard it is important to listen with both the ears and the mind.

Here are some points the leader should underscore when his people are to participate in discussions.

1.  Hear the other fellow out, don't interrupt. If your idea is any good, it will be just as good two or three minutes later.

126

2. Be brief and to the point; don't make long-winded speeches. If you're using reason rather than emotion only a few words are necessary.

3. Try to be as specific as possible; use examples.

4. Give the others the benefit of your experience. Speak freely and frankly.

5. Avoid hot arguments. Heat builds a barrier to objective group thinking and creates a wall.

The discussion leader will keep everyone in the group involved in the discussion and will discourage private conversations. When confusing points arise, he will see that they are clarified so that the group stays on the main track and the discussion continues to be focused.

One of the benefits of the conference is the training and motivating of subordinates by having them take part in what is today referred to as a participatory management, or giving employees the feeling that they are contributing to and participating in decisions.

### Managers Learn What Workers Want

When employees are involved in business decisions the manager benefits too because this relationship helps him get to know and evaluate his people.

Most supervisors are appallingly unaware of the things that are important to subordinates. For example, in a number of surveys supervisors who were asked to identify the first three motivational factors for employees ranked them in this order: (1) wages; (2) job security; (3) promotion and growth. The employees, however, in response to survey inquiries, ranked their first three job satisfaction factors as (1) full appreciation of work well done; (2) feeling "in" on things; (3) sympathetic help with problems.

127

It is interesting that with employees wages ranked fifth — and we certainly do not mean to imply by this fact that wages are unimportant. It is assumed that wages are appropriate for the job. Yet it is interesting to note that, in terms of job satisfaction or dissatisfaction relating directly to the quality of job performance and the final effectiveness of your operation, the interpersonal quality of the relationship has much greater impact upon the results than does the level of wages involved.

# Comparative Analysis of Well-Known Foodservice Operations

# 13

As you progress with your overall planning effort of developing a restaurant or foodservice facility, you are, no doubt, somewhat motivated by the thought that it was a bolt of genius that caused you to wake up one morning with this brilliant idea and by the feeling that our new operation will just have to succeed famously.

We have discussed in previous parts of this work the various types of foodservice operations and some of the factors affecting them; so perhaps it would be interesting to look at foodservice operations of various types and see what kind of sales are generated for each.

As we look at these operations, you should recognize that the sales figures examined in this chapter represent average sales and that there are some individual locations that do somewhat more and others that do a good deal less.

Without using individual company names, we will talk about specific companies and describe the category or type of foodservice operation with which each is involved.

As you look at the types of businesses listed on page 131, you see, with one or two exceptions, a fairly consistent level of sales in the area of $400,000 to $1,000,000 per year for a wide variety of restaurants. In other words, the fast-food, take-out restaurant gets into this level of sales as does the fine restaurant and some of the family restaurants.

If you stop looking after reaching this conclusion, the figures don't tell you much. However, in terms of equating this with the quality of your decision as to the direction that you want to do in your own effort, you might then analyze what kind of bottom line or net profit can be expected from these kinds of operations.

This requires analysis of the impact of: (1) capital invested in plant (building and equipment); (2) food costs (range from 36 percent to 48 percent; (3) labor costs; (4) hours of operation.

A restaurant operating from seven in the morning until three in the afternoon, serving breakfast and lunch in a relatively austere facility, and generating $750,000 in sales may well generate $125,000 to $150,000 in gross profit for its owner/operator. Not bad!

A more ostentatious restaurant, operating from eleven in the morning until one in the morning, generating $1,000,000 in sales, with a salaried manager, and corporate overhead allocation may well have difficulty attaining the same level of gross profit.

## TABLE 1
## ANALYSIS OF OPERATIONS     1974

| Type of Foodservice Operated | Average Sales Generated per Unit | |
|---|---|---|
| Fried Chicken Take-Out | $ 280,000 | Per yr. |
| Hamburger Chain | 397,000 | " " |
| Combination Sit-Down Restaurant and Lunch Counter | 464,000 | " " |
| Root Beer; Hot Dog Take-Out | 104.000 | " " |
| Hamburger, Fast-Food Take-Out | 304,000 | " " |
| Soft Ice Cream & Hamburgers Take-Out | 154,000 | " " |
| Hamburger, Take-Out | 394,000 | " " |
| Sit-Down Lunch Counter | 156,000 | " . " |
| Quality Family Restaurant— Sit-down, Using Convenience Foods | 901,000 | " " |
| Donuts and Limited Short Order | 264,000 | " " |
| Family Sit-Down Cafeteria | 375,000 | " " |
| Pizza | 276,000 | " " |
| Sit-Down, Short Order | 542,000 | " " |
| Public Cafeteria | 392,000 | " " |
| Family Sit-Down Restaurant | 509,000 | " " |
| Hot Dog Specialty, Fast-Food | 236,000 | " " |
| High Level, Quality Personality Restaurant | 1,350,000 | " " |
| Family Sit-Down Steak House | 2,000,000 | " " |
| Fast Service, Inexpensive Steaks Family Service | 829,000 | " " |
| Fine, High Quality Restaurant | 1,250,000 | " " |
| Quality Seafood Family Restaurant | 1,525,000 | " " |
| Fine Restaurant, Family & Business People | 910,000 | " " |

### Fast-Food, Take-Out

When you look at the fast-food and take-out operation, it is interesting to note the relationship of product cost to price, since the sales we have listed represent a high level of sales while the product cost may represent a high ratio of the sales when compared with product cost in other types of operations. It is also necessary to look at the size and skill level of the staff required to generate the sales level involved. Obviously, the fast-food, burger take-out establishments listed, all well-known companies, do not require the same level of skill or number of people to generate sales in the area of one-half million dollars a year that are required by the fine restaurants.

In addition, the fine restaurant has other overhead costs such as china, silver, linen, and various accessories that contribute to its overhead; the take-out establishment does not have these costs. It is also true that the average unit sale in the fine restaurant represents a higher figure; in other words, the check average is higher per person than it is in the fast-food restaurant. Those operations in the family sit-down category represent a situation somewhere between the two just discussed.

You will, therefore, want to review the figures illustrated here from the point of view of relating your investment, your food costs, your labor cost, your miscellaneous expenditures, depreciation of your building and equipment, taxes, and all other expenses to a bottom line at a realistic sales level. In doing so, you can determine the direction or course of action that will best meet your objectives as to profitability and return on investment.

You may wonder where you stand in terms of competing with the big names in the business; but remember that in this regard, it's just a matter of positive thinking if you follow proper planning techniques. To succeed, first you have to set a definite goal for yourself and a time by which you intend to achieve your goal.

132

Break your mental sound barrier because much of what you accomplish is more a matter of your mental conditioning than of any other factor. When Roger Bannister broke the 4-minute mile record, he said that this feat was accomplished more because of mental attitude than of physical condition. He set out to run the first three quarters in less than three minutes; he knew that if he could accomplish that much, he would automatically run the last quarter in less than one minute.

You have to develop a motivated outlook based upon confidence—which is generated by having done your home-work and having your facts well in mind. Doubt about yourself or about your ability to get the job done will give way to confusion and worry; it will lead to procrastination—putting off decisions in the hope that the problems will take care of themselves or go away.

On the other hand, egotism or a status-seeking attitude, causing you to worry more about what others think of you than about the business at hand, can also be a pitfall. Loss of purpose, or an attitude where there is no vision or plan for proceeding, will herald the end of your career as opposed to its beginning.

When you assess your ability to compete against the big names, it is encouraging to note that, according to the Depart-ment of Agriculture, 80 percent of the separate eating places in the United States are independently operated while approxi-mately 9 percent are franchised and a little more than 11 percent belong to multi-unit enterprises.

The table or booth "sit-down" type of restaurant is over-whelmingly independently operated—over 90 percent—and the counter, "informal lunch" type of restaurant is also over-whelmingly independently operated—over 91 percent.

The highest percentage of food facilities in the franchised category are drive-ins and fast-food restaurants—just under 20 percent. Cafeterias and carryout restaurants, on the other hand, are more likely than any other establishments to belong to a multi-unit organization.

It is true that chain restaurants are taking a greater share of the restaurant market each year, since in 1960 they accounted for a little over 6 percent of the total market, although they made up only 3 percent of all restaurants, whereas in 1968 they captured almost 10 percent of the total restaurant dollar and in 1978 almost 26 percent.

Part of this is the confidence in referral or carry-over attitude that exists. However, in looking at the individual restaurant, and particularly the atmosphere or family, sit-down type of restaurant, we find that throughout the country the most successful among such establishments are still almost invariably owned and operated by entrepreneurs. Sometimes, however, there are branches at three of four locations.

An analysis of the size of the chain restaurant company indicates that size does not seem to influence sales volume; in other words, chains with smaller numbers of locations were able to compete on a par with the chains having large numbers of operations, provided the operation itself was run effectively.

### Competition from Major Companies

In recent years, there have emerged into the restaurant market elements of the business community that had previously evinced little or no interest in the market. Among these companies are large conglomerates as well as grocery chains and a variety of food manufacturers and packers. These companies have recognized that about 35 percent of the dollars spent on food are spent on food eaten away from home and that this segment is expected to increase by another percent or so within the next five years.

The effects of competition from major companies will grow more serious because of the impact of their buying power and similar factors. This impact will be felt most keenly

134

by those competing in the cafeteria and fast-food chain areas. These are more likely to be the areas of activity that will attract companies such as large grocery and food packaging chains.

On the other hand, it has been illustrated historically, time and time again, that the major organizations seldom have the ability to maintain a sufficiently entrepreneurial attitude within their own organizations to encourage the type of management attitudes and approaches needed to compete effectively at the family sit-down, quality restaurant level, against the entrepreneur.

## Best Slot for the Individual

There are countless examples of individual entrepreneurs in various sections of the country who are operating good family sit-down restaurants with very profitable results and running circles around big company competition. In some cases these individuals are often running the big company competition out of town.

It would appear then that the greatest advantage for the individual entrepreneur is in the family sit-down suburban-type of restaurant, with the possibility of the next most promising level being that of the somewhat extended menu, fast-food, sit-down and/or take-out type of establishment.

The least attractive area for the individual entrepreneur would appear to be facilities associated with non-chain affiliated hotels/motels since the chain hotel/motel has a clear, overwhelming advantage in this sector.

It would then seem that the well-thought-out restaurant or food operation, or the extended menu, fast-food operation presented in a family atmosphere can be successful and provide an excellent return on investment as well as desired annual profit, provided the operation is assembled on the basis that total land and cost of building and equipment (the total

135

cost of a turnkey, ready-to-open facility) does not exceed a realistic equivalent of one year's sales.

To accomplish this goal, cost of land, facility, and building on a combined basis should not exceed $100 per foot—or better yet, should be somewhere between $3000 and $5000 per seat.

The relationship of the total cost to either of these two criteria would seem to indicate that, with a limited expenditure consistent with the expectations for the establishment and a satisfactory location, the operator can count on successful results despite competition from better known operations.

In the case of the intimate, family, sit-down type of restaurant, provided it is run effectively, competition from well-known organizations need not be a factor.

# The Future -
# What Lies Ahead?

# 14

The decade of the eighties will be amazing in many ways. Success will require managers to plan ahead and to perceive the fundamental adjustments taking place in our economy and in our way of doing things. This sort of planning and foresight will be especially important in areas of high capital intensive investment or improvement.

As indications of what to look for, we would like to point out a number of things that will undoubtedly greatly affect the whole course of commerce, and for that matter, our standard of living, during the next ten years or so. Some of the problems, such as potential shortages of conventional energy, are fairly obvious. The solutions to these problems may be more elusive, however.

137

Petroleum will continue to become both scarce and costly. This serious problem will be exacerbated by the increased presence, likely all of the way to the Arabian Gulf, of the Soviet Union, and reluctance of countries under its influence to rock the boat. This situation has awesome implications from the point of view of national security and national defense, as well as the position of the United States as a world power. It has equally significant implications for corporate planners.

Nuclear power will have to become a principal means of propulsion for naval vessels and you will probably see the use of voltaic cells emerge as the principal source of generated electricity for individual homes and buildings.

As a matter of fact, this author believes that solar voltaic cells will be produced as generating arrays for installation on individual homes, small businesses, and even as a source of electric power for small, two-seat automobiles. In any event, energy utilization, sources, and conservation considerations will grow increasingly important in your planning of equipment and facilities.

Attitudes of customers and of employees alike will be another factor of great significance. There has been a convulsion in America over the past several years, and the reaction that is now setting in will be strong and far-reaching.

We have been through a period of self-indulgence and excess, and like those people in the Alka Seltzer ads, we now have indigestion. As a result, there is today a deep longing for the quiet of times gone by. There is a longing to become insulated from the hectic pressures which impose from every side, screeching out at us from the TV and newspaper headlines, frustrating us as we attempt to make our budgets cover necessities, glaring out at us from the signs in front of gas pumps as prices escalate, and on and on. There is a mood for nostalgia, and almost anything from the past has become a collectible.

The mood of nostalgia, the desire to escape from the screech of the world around us and from the economic pressures of inflation, coupled with shortages of energy, will likely emphasize and encourage a greater movement of population to rural areas. This trend will manifest itself not only in movement from urban and suburban to rural, but also in movement from northern cold climate areas and eastern congested areas to the South and West; and for the first time, even relatively uncrowded areas like the Pacific Northwest will feel the pressures that accompany population growth.

The music trend of the eighties will be reminiscent of that of the early forties. This softer, slower music is right in step with the nostalgia that is a natural reaction to the "psychological indigestion" our country is experiencing.

The traditions of courtesy and thoughtfulness will become more and more valued. People will seek a quiet, low-pressure atmosphere; service by the fireplace will be very much the vogue.

As the restaurant dining room becomes more atmospheric, the kitchen will become more efficient. Data-based cooking systems, involving a perforated card which goes into the slot on the radar range or similar appliance, will become very prominent in the field of fast-food, convenience food, and pre-prepared or pre-packaged entrees. This system will not only ensure quality control and uniformity, it will also fill the gap that is left when there are not enough well-trained and experienced people available for kitchen assignments.

National and world events will affect businesses. The mid-eighties will undoubtedly find our country in the precarious position of confrontation with other major powers and yet relatively helpless to react to such threats. The lack of interest in defense spending during the sixties and early seventies has resulted in decreased military strength. Now, in the eighties, this chicken is coming home to roost.

Therefore, we can expect that the national mood will, as a matter of necessity, turn inward. The direction of political thought will be toward relative isolationism and "fortress America." Given the extreme interdependence of the various monetary systems of the world today, this inward-looking attitude will necessarily create severe problems for the economy.

Capital formation, acceptable costs for money, availability of credit, and even the methods and criteria for extending credit, will require major revision and adjustment. Variable interest rates, which are tied to the prime rate and keep adjusting with it, will be a good deal more prevalent than they were in the past. The practice of including, as a part of the lending arrangement, options to take equity position, or equity positions outright, will emerge with increasing frequency.

Unionization will fall further behind in terms of size of membership. This trend will be the inevitable result of the fact that the federal government, through OSHA, unemployment compensation, National Labor Relations, the Department of Labor, social security, and so on, has eliminated, for the most part, the causes upon which the existence of unions depends. Workers will increasingly want to know what is in it for them and the answer will not be favorable for a resurgence of unionism.

Basic tastes in food, however, will remain fairly constant. The tastes described in the first edition of this book, published in the early seventies, have not changed appreciably, nor will they change in the eighties.

Success will require alertness to what is going on around you, particularly with respect to major trends. The alert, informed, and well-prepared entrepreneur need not fear the major corporation, but he does need to be more careful in

140

setting up his operation. The entrepreneur, however, rarely has the staying power of the major corporation; he cannot afford to operate in the red for long periods while his restaurant slowly takes hold. As we said, at the very beginning of this book, THE PLAN IS THE THING.

## Changing American Values

Throughout the years, efforts on the part of the foodservice operations and restaurants have in too many cases become stereotyped and progressively dull.

Food has become more and more uniform and unimaginative. Efforts to outdo the competitor have been gauged either purely by price considerations, with little relationship to value offered, or by gimmicks.

Despite protestations to the contrary, very seldom has true, in-depth evaluation of the customer and his desires provided the basis for either product development or product improvement.

Furthermore, competitive pressures have resulted in the generation of precooked, pre-prepared, frozen foods. This activity has largely been divided between the frozen food developer and the restaurateur, with the food developer not necessarily oriented to the restaurant customer and the restaurateur often automatically resisting this kind of food as substandard and therefore not acceptable in his restaurant.

An entirely different orientation to and depth of analysis of this market will be necessary in the future if success for a foodservice operation is to be assured. No longer will it be sufficient to plaster the name of a celebrity on the sign out front, or to use gimmicky containers that make the portions look larger than they really are.

141

We are the first civilization to find itself on the threshold of a new experience for man; the post-industrial era. We are beginning to see in consumer attitudes some of the manifestations of this experience.

Primitive nations had the ability to produce from the soil as they passed through and emerged from the agrarian phase and reached the point where simple mechanization and rudimentary industrialization began to take place.

As other nations moved thrugh the industrial phase they became more affluent as they developed the ability to produce more than could be consumed at home. This is particularly true of the advanced nations, especially the United States. As advanced nations moved through the advanced industrial phase to the post-industrial phase, they moved from a society based upon survival needs to one based upon personal choice. Barring a catastrophe, our rate of development within the next twenty years appears to be well on the way to a gross national product of twice the current level and an output per man-hour that will probably double, as labor and management alike find it necessary to draw together to improve quality control and productivity.

This shift will permit a much larger portion of the energy and resources of the nation to move to non-economic areas that people feel are important. For the first time, we will be a nation with the opportunity to produce better people instead of better products.

To produce better people, however, will require better products. Marketing management will have to change as will foodservice management and restaurateurs. Instead of pursuing the value strategies of the past, they will have to turn to ecological strategies and considerations as well as to aesthetic strategies and considerations in the future. This new direction will be borne upon a strange combination of technology and nostalgia.

142

Transcontinental travel and intercontinental travel will no doubt give way to a more regionalized existence. While people will not give up their yen to travel, they will tend to travel shorter distances, in more regional patterns.

These trends, then, in conjunction with the demographic data in earlier chapters, give us an insight into future problems and a direction for long-range planning. Clearly this insight and planning must be tied to an understanding of future values and the way they will affect what people want and how people will be motivated.

### Value Patterns

Among people, values are more stable over the long run than any other personality variable except the IQ. In order to determine value changes, broad patterns held in common by large segments of the population have to be identified, as values tend to be related to the basic needs people have.

Human values are as old as man's existence; and various anthropologists and psychologists have used different terms to define the same things; "protection," "support," "security," "basic trust," and "survival" are all used more or less synonymously.

The primary level of human need is survival. Survival needs are tied primarily to environment and include basic requirements of sleep, food, drink, shelter. These needs have the greatest impact upon the conduct of people, for as Gandhi once said, "To the poor man, God must appear in the form of bread."

At the poverty level, survival needs represent the dominant concern of people. Survival needs spawn attitudes of selfishness, distrust, instability, and resentment toward those "better off." Usually people are at this level because of a deprived upbringing or severe poverty or the absence of opportunity.

After emerging from the survival level of need, the next level becomes the "security" level. People at this level have to feel protected from physical, economic, and other types of catastrophes. This level is typified by a feeling of insecurity, fear of making decisions, and a suspicion of and resistance to new or changing conditions.

People with these needs want a strong leader and will give almost anything for law and order. They will usually fight only when cornered and often are found among minorities, people with small businesses, the poor, "outside" groups.

Rising to the next level, people acquire the need for "belonging." This need is exemplified in their drive to be part of something bigger, to love and to be loved, to be a part of the group, to have roots somewhere and to care about something outside of one's self. It is also exemplified in conformist, matriarchal attitudes, the need to be popular, and belief in safety in numbers.

People at this level usually prefer a great number of acquaintances to a few deep friendships. They are status quo-oriented, non-experimental, gossipy, stereotyped, and greatly dependent upon the opinions of others. These individuals also find it hard to say no. They are often found among organization men, middle-class joiners, and happy housing-development dwellers.

Next, one is faced with the "esteem" level of need where the dominant value becomes achievement, often referred to as "success." Here the need is for others to "think well of you." The key need of the "belonger" is to fit in, whereas the key need of the "esteemer" is to stand out. A person at this level is materialistic, power-oriented, status-seeking, risk-taking, and hard-driving.

Normally, people having needs at this level go through two phases. The first is that of attaining the esteem of others, and then from there they go on to develop self-esteem. The whole world is viewed as a contest arena. This level is often represented by individuals such as business executives and politicians.

### Self-Actualization

The one level, which does not necessarily identify itself with any particular economic stratification but which is the upper level of need, is the "self-actualization" level. The key here is living up to one's inner potential. The self-actualizer is a mature person, able to express himself fully in the total range of his abilities in a way that is peculiarly his. Men and women who reach this level are very individualistic, idealistic, creative, self-reliant, and flexible. They have a sense of mission as well as a wide range of varied interests. These individuals, interestingly enough, are found in every walk of life and in every occupation.

Individual characteristics are illustrated generally as social characteristics; however, from our viewpoint, each market expresses a level of need together with its associated values and resources. To identify with the consumer, it is necessary to identify needs, values, and resources as though they were operating in an interrelated sequence.

Each market is seeking gratification at its appropriate level. Identification of values helps (1) reveal the course that will best satisfy the need and (2) introduce the elements to do so.

As we consider the demographics that have been presented previously, the increase in realization of the "esteem" level — and, in fact, the "self-actualization" level as it imparts its pressures in the ecological, conservation, and aesthetic

145

areas, we are going to find a requirement to get away from garish buildings (the McDonald remodeling trend is a good example of a step in this direction) and to present a wider variety of choice made available in a satisfying, if not uplifting, atmosphere.

### Buying Needs

At the "survival" level the problem is quite simple, with buying needs opposing resources. Historical measuring devices for following these ideas at more complex levels have included comparisons of spending profiles in relation to income levels and family size. The historic measuring devices might be enhanced and have a greater impact if modified to examine changes in spending habits as a large family of five or six shrinks to a smaller family of three or four, without a change in income.

This will indicate the relative role of values at the "security," "belonging," and "esteem" levels, because it will indicate priority shifts resulting from greater discretionary income, but without the benefit of long-term higher family income.

For example, today people making less than $5,000 per year tend to be in the "security" or "survival" level, whereas those with $10,000 to $12,000 tend to be in the "belonging" level; and earners of $15,000 and above tend to be at the "esteem" level. The average education of the "security" group is about ten years of schooling, with about twelve years for those in the "belonging" group, and fourteen years or more at the "esteem" level.

As "esteem" level needs are satisfied, there appears marked departures from the spending patterns of the other levels. Consequently, as segments of the population move from one need level to another and are identified, it may be anticipated that a pattern tending to self-actualization will emerge. This will be particularly so if this upward movement is

146

brought about as a result of successful, individual efforts, aided and abetted by training and opportunity.

If, on the other hand, the changes come about as a result of subsidies and guaranteed income, the future spending patterns could be quite different.

"Belonging" families spend more on a wider range of choices than do "security" families. Choices made on spending relate to the way people view themselves and wish others to view them. In terms of priority of interest, personal image ranks very high whereas local transportation and home expenses rank the lowest. These choices are made on the basis of the visibility of the results to others.

As the number of consumers in the higher income levels increases, future consumers will follow different life-styles and this change will influence the course we must follow if we are to attract these consumers to our particular establishments.

Youngsters today are taking off from a benchmark of present family attainment levels and can reasonably be expected to move to still higher standards. The change in the population mix at the "esteem" level, probably most contributed to by higher educational level averages, is most significant.

For many at this level, income is not necessarily a goal in itself but rather a means or vehicle for attaining the trappings that contribute to satisfaction of the "esteem" need. For example, travel as an item of leisure spending has a very high order of priority. It will pay to know the kinds of choices that will be made by "esteemers."

Some consumers at these levels are encouraged to acquire items by perceiving them as necessities rather than as luxuries. Look at the way the second car has become a necessity for those at this level. Food away from home satisfies the "esteem urge," so does private education for one's children.

As more people make the transition from the belonging level to the esteem level, expenditures for food eaten away from home will, as they are already doing, tend to increase as a ratio of total food expenditures.

It must be recognized, however, that as this transition to higher need levels is realized by more consumers, food away from home, as now offered, will not satisfy the consumer requirement. The trend will be toward more attractively prepared, flavorful food offerings, with a wider variety of choice. Further, this food must be served in an atmosphere that does not clash to an offensive degree with the environment but instead contributes to the diner's feelings of self-esteem and self-actualization. These factors will become very significant in the competitive patterns.

The impact of high production capacity, improvement in the level of average education, as well as the income level, upon discretionary spending priorities would indicate an amazing growth in the so-called service industries. It is not at all unlikely that within twenty years two-thirds of all jobs in the United States will be in the service industries—with a major input into the so-called leisure, travel, and "food away from home" segments.

Recognition of these factors should become a significant cornerstone in building a successful pattern in the restaurant marketplace during the next several years.

Significant among the declining values requiring new responses from the foodservice industry are bland foods and the urge to group conformity. They have been replaced by new interest in flavor and respect for individual standards.

The change in values projected among future customers will require variety, interesting presentation, emphasis on flavor, and an opportunity to exercise freedom of choice. These goals must be carefully structured within a format that is economically sound as well as satisfying to customers.

## The Other Side of the Mountain

Back to basics for a moment. Let us review what has occurred over the past thirty-five years, and its impact as well as implications for the long-range future.

From 1947 to 1957 we experienced the largest "baby boom" in our history; approximately 30,000,000 youngsters came into the world. Mistaking this increase for a trend, we overbuilt schools, and later, we overbuilt colleges. We trained large numbers of teachers and assembled a massive administrative structure for education. This population aberration progressively generated several crises, primarily because of our defective perception as to what was really happening.

The population pyramid may be seen as a train running along the track of history. Each generation produces a load to be carried from the origin (birth) to the destination (death).

Our vantage point may be likened to a station platform from which we view each car as it passes and draw conclusions about the load being carried. In this case we saw the loads first diminish slightly, then increase dramatically with the baby boom. We did not perceive, nor did we anticipate, that later cars on the train would in fact have dramatically smaller loads.

This is most significant, and particularly critical at present, since one must recognize that babies become young children, school children, young adults, mature adults, middle-aged adults, and finally, aged adults.

The folk in each of these categories have different needs and progressively different values, according to their position on the population pyramid. Our focus upon the baby boom aberration as it moved through the initial steps of progression caused us to assume that values were likewise changing in fundamental ways. This assumption is naive, in the light of history.

149

History indicates that as blocks of individuals move up the population pyramid (these blocks are known by demographers as *cohorts*) they have predictable impact.

For example, an unusually large cohort first produces a boom in the diaper business, followed by a boom in the tricycle business, a boom in the bicycle business, a boom in the automobile business, a boom in the need for apartments, and a boom in the need for houses.

History also shows that as a larger cohort imposes its demands upon the economy (supply) it strains the supply and produces growth. If the strain is great and quickly imposed over a short time, it also produces inflation. This is because the economy of the United States requires delicate balance between the supply side (production capacity) and the demand side. If this is not recognized, the danger is that supply may be overstimulated in any given stage of demand. Then as that peak demand passes, the sharp reduction leaves us with overdeveloped supply. Rapid retrenchment follows, invariably characterized by layoffs, unemployment, and so forth.

The fact is that the cars on our railroad that have followed those carrying the baby boom have had sharply reduced loads. The average family has shrunk from 4.7 to a little over three persons. This means that the total family income divided by the number of family members results in more income (per person) to spend. However, with the large size of this particular age group, it also means more adults to compete, and as history has shown, less opportunity, and a greater tendency to be insecure and to "play it safe."

People in this group, now in the 23 to 33 age band and pressing for housing, are undergoing significant emotional experiences as they deal with "survival" for the first time. Since they were able to start at the esteem level, skipping over the survival and shelter levels because of family attitudes, they are now finding it necessary to reassess and adjust their values.

150

It is inevitable that the 1980s will bring on a major housing boom. With a housing boom will come concurrent booms in furniture, appliances, and other home accessories. However, as this group continues into old age it is being followed by a much smaller cohort, which will find more opportunity, and more rapid advancement because there will be fewer people to fill the available jobs.

This smaller component of population will have to face, and solve, the dilemma of overbuilt production capacity, overbuilt institutions, and overbuilt government bureaucracy. If we anticipate this significant condition at the turn of the century, we can begin earlier to trim institutions geared to accommodating much larger numbers. We can also develop the ability to compete overseas (particularly in China, South America, and Africa) where enormous demand will provide a means for us to avoid major economic collapse by virtue of substantial export. If we are prepared with this type of planning, the road just over the crest of the mountain will be easy. If not, we will be faced with major depressionary forces, and the real possibility of major economic collapse.

If, during the boom of the eighties and nineties, we maintain the delicate balance between supply and demand through carefully staged stimulation, we can avoid major increases in inflation. Tax relief designed to stimulate supply must precede stimulus to demand.

We must begin to perceive events in the context of waves of the future, as opposed to hypnotic focus on the surface ripples of today.

The road forks with more serious potential consequence than ever before in our history. Only in that period just prior to the Great Depression, when a collapse of the demand side destroyed support for production and jobs, was the future more grave.

151

The corporate planner must be perceptive, indeed. He must throw off his historical disdain for political activism, and must make enlightened positions felt in the halls of government, corporation board rooms, and union meeting halls.

For the manager in the foodservice field, the format of his restaurant, the selections on his menu, and the thrust of his marketing effort must track with the movement of the population in his market through the population pyramid.

Rigidity and short-range planning will be sure paths to disaster in an industry where there exists, historically, the highest rate of bankruptcies. If you are to be successful, you must not think only about decor and food, but also think about market identification and demographics. You must be sensitive to what is happening, perceptive to its implications, and you must posture your operation to be "with it."

# APPENDIX:

# Flow Diagrams and Planning Guide

The flow diagrams provided in this guide provide for organization of systems for (a) cost control, (b) inventory control, and (c) plant layout. They are arranged in appropriate sequence for outlining the planning evolution, beginning with The Basic System.

153

## The Basic System

Raw materials requirements are determined by these steps:

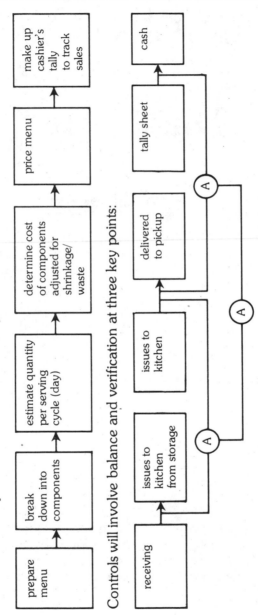

| prepare menu | → | break down into components | → | estimate quantity per serving cycle (day) | → | determine cost of components adjusted for shrinkage/waste | → | price menu | → | make up cashier's tally to track sales |

Controls will involve balance and verification at three key points:

| receiving | → | issues to kitchen from storage | → | issues to kitchen | → | delivered to pickup | → | tally sheet | → | cash |

With reconciliation points A between stages.

Reconciliations at points indicated by an A will establish control and will isolate problems.

The diagram below illustrates flow of materials through the three basic departments of every restaurant and food operation. Those departments are: (a) steward, (b) kitchen, and (c) sales, or dining room. In small operations one individual may occupy more than one position.

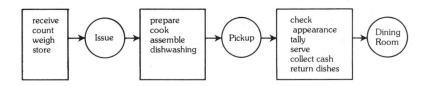

Comparing this with the diagram on the facing page, one can determine, in general, the processes required, the equipment needed (size and amount), the space required, and the number of employees.

Now you are ready to efficiently arrange equipment according to flow of materials, processes, and traffic patterns.

Actual space requirements can now be estimated for each department (functional area) of the operation.

## Steward: Receiving and storage

| Receiving: | Storage: |
|---|---|
| counting | refrigerated |
| weighing | freezer |
| recording | dry storage |
| | paper and linen |

## Production: Kitchen

cleaning and preparation
cooking, frying, baking, broiling
assembly
dishwashing

## Sales: Dining room

quality check of food going into dining room
appearance and temperature
tally of items sold, for food cost/cash control
collection of cash
supervision of waitresses/waiters
seating of customers
cleanliness and appearance of public areas
customer complaints

Given a starting point of a specific number of seats, such as a 160-seat restaurant, you can now determine fairly accurately the space required.

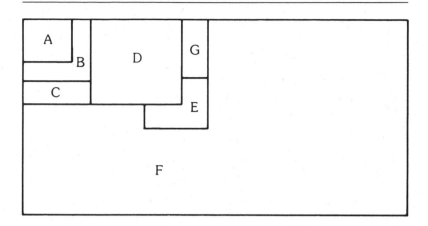

Space can be correlated to obtain efficiency of design. In the above illustration A is receiving; B is storage and refrigeration; C is the employee dressing room, etc.; D is for preparation, cooking, assembly, and delivery (main kitchen); E is waitress pick up and cashier's check point, and F is public area, for dining, etc. G illustrates the way in which public restrooms, and the like, can be situated to "round out" the layout.

In this instance we end up with a basic rectangular building (economical to build). Back of the house area is about 20% to a maximum of 30% of the total area. Poor planning of space utilization and flow may often result in ratio of back of house to front of house such as 40 or 45% to 50 or 55%.

# Index

163

# About the Author

Dewey A. Dyer bases the recommendations in this book on twenty years of varied experience which has earned him a reputation as a "can do" innovator and a number of "first-use" credits as well.

## Foodservice

- direction—as division vice-president with responsibility for food facilities—of operations ranging from fine restaurants and clubs to recreational facilities and from concessions in stadiums and sports arenas throughout the United States to special-event catering.

167

- overall supervision of industrial feeding for over 40,000 employees of a leading electronic manufacturing company.

## Construction

- Senior vice-president of a major consortium engaged in the design and development of extensive housing, commercial buildings, port facilities, and related transport and logistics systems in Alaska and elsewhere.

- registered professional engineer engaged directly, and as a consultant, in the design of a wide range of facilities including supervision of construction and remodeling as well as operation of completed food, recreation, and hospitality facilities.

## Equipment

- early association with the development of microwave cooking techniques.

- managing director of equipment manufacturing division.

## Management

- active as consultant in various business endeavors involving education, training, marketing, and finance.

- successful writer about techniques of management.

168